Mother Teresa's
Reaching Out
in Love

Mother Teresa's Reaching Out in Love

Stories told by Mother Teresa

Original title: *Reaching Out in Love*

Compiled and Edited by
Edward Le Joly and Jaya Chaliha

BARNES & NOBLE

NEW YORK

Lord, make me an instrument of Your peace
Where there is hatred, let me sow love;
Where there is injury, pardon;
Where there is doubt, faith;
Where there is despair, hope;
Where there is darkness, light;
Where there is sadness, joy.

O Divine Master, grant that I may not so much
seek to be consoled as to console;
To be understood as to understand;
To be loved as to love;
For it is in giving that we receive;
It is in pardoning that we are pardoned;
And it is in dying that we are born to eternal life.

—Prayer for Peace of Saint Francis of Assisi

Contents

Mother Teresa Speaks

*H*ow do you speak, Mother?' a friend asked.

She said: 'I make a little cross on my lips with my thumb. Then I stand up, I look straight before me, above the crowd and I deliver my message.'

During her long speaking career Mother spoke on countless occasions in over a hundred countries over four decades. She talked to people belonging to all classes of society and all religious beliefs.

What she said was concrete, and since she always made it a point to observe the local people and their living conditions, her talks were adapted to her listeners.

Mother used no notes, no paper for her speeches. She did not write out her speeches. She knew what she wanted to say. Her message was usually adorned with two or three little stories of her experiences and never too long.

Mother Teresa wrote nothing for publication, though she gave many recorded interviews. In her talks, messages and addresses she told little stories she had experienced or witnessed. In the stories gathered in this book the readers will find both wit and wisdom. While wit is of the earth, wisdom is of heaven—wit is human, wisdom divine, a gift of God. A witty word, short and snappy, draws a smile and is remembered. A wise saying enriches, comforts and elevates. Mother provides wit with measure, wisdom in abundance.

Some stories short and easy to remember were frequently told by Mother. For instance, the dying man in the Kalighat home who said, 'I lived like an animal, I die like an angel.' And the story about the lonely man in Melbourne who would not light his beautiful lamp in the evening because nobody ever visited him.

Some stories were pathetic. Once Mother saw a child eating a piece of bread she had given him crumb by crumb because, he said, 'When the bread is over I shall be hungry again.'

Some stories were distressing, a blame on modern society as Mother attacked abortion and mentioned what the Sisters were doing to help unwed mothers and save unwanted children.

A few stories Mother told only to intimate friends. They showed her zeal for souls in a beautiful light and her commanding courage.

After receiving the Nobel Peace Prize in Oslo in 1979 she was invited to several receptions in India. The first one was of course in Calcutta. It took place in a public park able to accommodate a large crowd. For her it was like playing on your home ground where everybody knows you, loves you, cheers you.

The chief minister presided and several ministers were also present. Mother had her seat next to the chief minister. Welcoming the Nobel Peace Prize Laureate, the chief minister said how proud Calcutta was to have her. Then he stated that in a communist state concern for the welfare of the poor and needy is the duty of the state. But since this state was not able to fulfil its responsibilities entirely, Mother Teresa and her Sisters were welcome to help. He went on to praise their work and promised his support.

Mother replied, 'I wish to say that every person must be concerned with the welfare of his neighbours. It is a duty of charity. We must show our love for all men and women who are God's children and, so, are our brothers and sisters.'

Mother's talks always had a purpose and a message. At the core of Mother's message was love for God and for all God's children.

How is love obtained?

At times Mother inserted in her letters a small printed card stating:

> *Without prayer no faith*
> *Without faith no love*
> *Without love no service*
> *Without service no joy, no peace.*

Thus there are four essential steps—Prayer, Faith, Love and Action—resulting in interior joy and peace in society. To obtain this result there is a preliminary condition: prayer requires interior and exterior silence. Silence of the eyes, of the ears, of the mind, of the imagination. One has to be self-composed, able to concentrate, open to God's inspiration. For exterior silence in noisy towns and cities one needs to find a quiet corner in a room or a park.

A great apostle of prayer, Mother was frequently seen

fingering her rosary beads even while travelling. At public meetings she repeatedly invited people to pray.

On most solemn occasions with heads of states and society leaders she took the initiative to lead the audience in prayer. The two most famous occasions were at Oslo when receiving the Nobel Peace Prize and in New York in the Assembly Hall of the UN for its fortieth anniversary celebrations. She took the initiative and led the audience in reciting the Prayer for Peace of Saint Francis of Assisi. Her friends had distributed leaflets with the prayer, as she had planned in advance.

Mother advocated family prayers as a way to keep a family united and happy. She popularised the slogan coined by Father Peyton: 'The family that prays together stays together.' Mother Teresa made the slogan her own and proclaimed it all over the world.

Once, as Mother was inspecting the tiny babies at Shishu Bhavan, the children's home in Calcutta, a Sister told her sadly, 'This baby is dying.' Mother said, 'Let us recite the Lord's Prayer together.' They did, and Mother carried on her inspection. Three hours later, the Sister reported, 'The sickly child is saved.' Such incidents happened several times over the years. Mother did not work miracles; she just prayed and Jesus responded.

To a Japanese editor who said that he did not believe in God, Mother said, 'Go down on your knees and say, "My God, I believe in you, I love you. My God, I trust you. I am sorry for my sins." Then do some small things with great love.'

To a volunteer who told her he had lost his faith she

gave a book of prayer. He came back after three weeks and said, 'Now I believe.'

Mother impressed her Sisters by her faith and her trust in God. She never doubted her call and the support of God to her Society. At the beginning, when she started without money, without a house, without members, with no official backing or support, it required heroism. Yet she says: 'From the start of our Congregation I never doubted that it was God's work, that it would succeed. But I did not think that it would become so big. It is all God's work.'

Her trust in God's Providence was such that she refused monthly allowances offered to her Sisters in New York and in Montreal, among other places. She feared that if she accepted, 'the Sisters would lose their trust in God and the joy of depending entirely on God's Providence.'

Mother said that faith is essential to realize the dignity of every man and woman created by God. Faith should not be affected by suffering for only faith can give suffering a meaning. Mother had a word of consolation for persons who suffer, as she says: 'Suffering opens up space within that otherwise would not be there—so that God can come in and fill it.' Having suffered much herself, she said: 'God made me a big grace: he sent me suffering.' As a result, she could be detached from all human consolation and was completely open to God's presence and action—like Jesus dying on the cross. She suffered three heart attacks. For the first one she stayed in a Roman hospital for one month. For the second one she was admitted to a Calcutta nursing home for six weeks. After recovery, she started travelling and speaking all over the world. The third one brought her close to death. Again she recovered well enough to travel to Rome and the United States.

The core of Mother Teresa's message was love. Love God and love one another.

She said, 'We cannot show our love for God whom we cannot see and who is in need of nothing except by loving and serving our neighbour whom we see and love as God's child.

'Without love there can be no happiness in the house, no peace in the world. A work of love is a work of peace.'

In her talks and writings, Mother developed two great principles: Holiness is for all; and charity begins at home.

Mother had a purpose to fulfil through these ideas. She wanted to make people better, more loving, more generous, more faithful, more devoted, in one word—more holy. She preached and repeated to persons of all religions: be holy as God is holy. Mother confessed: 'Often when I tell them holiness is for all, is for them, they are astonished. They thought that holiness is only for priests and nuns, the professionals of religion.'

She explained that holiness means to do our vocation perfectly, what we are expected to do. A doctor, a teacher, a businessman, a farmer, a housewife, a student are called to be holy in accordance with their positions in life. This message was both consoling and challenging.

She also said that love is first to be experienced in the family. The happiness of the family depends mostly on the woman. She is the heart of the home. And Mother gives practical advice for a happy family life—'Smile.'

After the home comes the neighbourhood. Mother insisted, 'There are poor people everywhere. To be unwanted, lonely and unloved is worse than to be hungry. Even in well-to-do neighbourhoods you find cases of lonely people. Visit them. Cheer them up.'

She said, 'Some people wrote to me they wished to come and work as volunteers in Calcutta. I wrote back: "No need to come to Calcutta. Start working in your own country. Begin in your house, in your neighbourhood, in your town or village, in your district. Discover the people in need of spiritual or material help. In some countries of Asia and Africa there is mostly material poverty; but in the rich countries of Europe and America there is much spiritual poverty and it is more difficult to cure."'

Cheerfulness as a sign of love was one of the main characteristics of Mother Teresa and her Missionaries of Charity. She wanted all her Sisters to be cheerful and gave the example herself. She brought happiness and life wherever she went.

Mother said, 'Be smiling when you visit the poor. Even if you have nothing to give, smile to them; a smile costs nothing.'

Some volunteers who came to work among the poor for a few weeks or months confessed that at the beginning they could not sleep. 'After seeing so much misery, so much suffering during the whole day, when I went to bed at night, I cried and cried and could not sleep,' so each one said. What about the Sisters who see and touch misery during their whole lives? Mother, foreseeing this danger advised the Sisters: 'Whatever misery, whatever suffering you have seen and experienced during the day, never go to bed without the joy of the Risen Christ.'

Another characteristic of Mother was her decisiveness. She always advocated immediate action. She would never temporise or dilly-dally. She agreed with Winston Churchill who during the war had on his desk a plaque on which was inscribed, 'Action Today.' To her Sisters she said repeatedly: 'Yesterday is past, tomorrow may never come, we have only today to work for Jesus.'

Mother recalled that the first interview she accepted was at Malcolm Muggeridge's request, for the BBC. The interview was broadcast all over England. Muggeridge later followed up with a film he shot in Calcutta. The television crew were preparing to shoot the film showing Mother Teresa and her Sisters at work in Mother House. As the Sisters gathered in the open courtyard, Mother issued an unforgettable clarion call: 'Let us do something beautiful for God.'

This summed up the whole of her life.

The authors have tried to do just that as they present to the reader the BEST of Mother Teresa's stories as she told them.

Calcutta   Edward Le Joly, SJ
March 1998

Mother Teresa

A chart hung on the wall of the parlour in Mother House, Calcutta—

> *Agnes Bojaxhiu*
> *Daughter of Nicholas and Rosa*
> *Younger sister to Agatha and Lazarus*
> *Born on August 26, 1910 at Skolpje*
> *Baptised on August 27, 1910.*

Brother Janez Udovc, who was serving in the church of the town at the time remembered:

'Agnes's family was very religious. She herself had a fine voice; she was really our prima donna, the soprano soloist of the parish choir. She also directed the choir in the absence of the choirmaster.'

At the age of twelve years, young Agnes—Teresa was her religious name—expressed her wish to her mother, Rosa: 'I would very much like to be a nun.' Rosa told her that she must wait till she was older.

As a teenager, Agnes read a news item sent by a Yugoslavian Jesuit priest in Bengal, asking for candidates willing to work in India. When she was eighteen years old, she felt the 'call' had come for her to follow her vocation and on 26 September 1928, she left home and went to Dublin to join the community of Loreto nuns as a novice. Two months later she was on her way to India. She arrived at Howrah station, one of the two major railway stations in Calcutta, on 6 January 1929.

Her second 'call within a call' to start a new institute to work among the poorest of the poor came on 10 September 1947.

Mother Teresa was the foundress of the Missionaries of Charity which received the official nod from the Vatican on 7 October 1950.

Saint of the Slums

$\mathcal{M}$other Teresa went to work in the slums in 1948. Thereafter she and her Sisters became familiar figures in some of the most depressed and deprived areas of the world. In the early years, she had no car of her own and used the public transport system. Until she allowed herself to be dissuaded from doing so for reasons of health and age, Mother often used to walk to her place of work in the slums and ghettos of the world. She herself was very observant and would exhort her Sisters: 'Open your eyes and see.'

This is a story she vividly remembered and often repeated:

'I'll never forget one day I was walking down the street and saw something moving in the open drain. I removed the dirt and found a human being there. He had been eaten by worms and, after we had brought him to our house, it took us three hours to clean him. And this man—who lived such a terrible life of suffering in that open drain only said: "I have lived like an animal in the street, but I'm going to die like an angel, loved and cared for." And just as we were still praying with him, praying for him, he looked up at the Sister and said, "Sister, I'm going home to God," and he died. There was such a wonderful, beautiful smile on his face. I've never seen a smile like that.

'It was so wonderful to see the greatness of a man who could speak like that without complaining, without cursing. Like an angel! This is the greatness of people who are spiritually rich when they are materially poor.'

Slums in Heaven

*I*t was in her letters that the laughter which, with Mother Teresa, was never far away came over almost audibly—letters written in her bold handwriting late at night, in trains and on aeroplanes, on cheap notepaper or the insides of envelopes or scraps of paper.

Mother recalls in a letter from Calcutta how, in the very early days of her work there, she was confined to bed with a high fever and was delirious. 'In that delirium,' she wrote, 'I went to Saint Peter, but he did not let me enter saying, "There are no slums in heaven." In my anger, I said: "Very well, I will fill heaven with slum people and you will be forced to let me in." '

When Mother wrote this letter, the number of entrants to the Missionaries of Charity had grown to some hundreds and later she founded a Brotherhood also. Hence she wrote: 'Poor Saint Peter! Since then the Sisters and Brothers don't give him rest, and he has to be careful because our people have reserved their place in heaven long ago by their suffering.'

A Little Pencil

Mother described herself as a little pencil in God's hand—merely His instrument. She herself had to use a writing instrument a great deal in her daily administrative work of running the Missionaries of Charity all over the world. As the foundress and Superior General of her Order, her smallest act was a living example for her Sisters and those who worked with her. She used to say:

'I find that when I'm writing, writing and writing, I use up the pens so quickly. When the ink begins to look very faint, a Sister puts a new pen in my hand.' After Mother finished, she always returned the pen to the Sister because she said, 'I won't take anything without permission.'

'If I Had Just Passed By'

I could not have been a Missionary of Charity,' Mother Teresa told her Sisters, 'if I had passed by when I saw and smelt that woman who was eaten up by rats—her face, her legs. But I returned, picked her up and took her to a hospital. If I had not, the Society would have died. Feelings of repugnance are human but if I see the face of Jesus in his most distressing disguise, I will be holy.'

'We Do It For Jesus'

Women connected with other social welfare organizations often offered their services to Mother Teresa.

One woman said, 'We also do social work like you, Mother, and would like to help you.' Mother wanted them to be involved with her work but also wanted them to understand the true nature of her mission. She prefaced her explanation with:

'A clean heart can see God. And we should see God in each other. This is what Jesus taught us: "Love one another. You did it to me. That small thing, you did it to me."

'We are not social workers. We may be doing social work in the eyes of some people, but we do it for Jesus.'

Then, Mother gave this example:

'One day, one of our Sisters picked up a man from the street, and in lifting him up, his skin remained on the footpath. The Sister took him home but it took her a long time to care for him, for his body was full of worms. After two or three hours, he died with the most wonderful smile on his face. I asked that Sister: "What did you feel when you were touching that body? When you were touching so closely?"

'She said: "Mother, I've never before felt the presence of Christ, but really, really, I was sure, I was touching his body." '

A Home For Leprosy Patients

The work for the leprosy patients at the Titagarh Leprosy Home,' said Mother on the occasion of its jubilee, 'was from the very start one of our main works.'

Mother received the Templeton Prize for Progress in Religion in 1973 and with the money she was able to consolidate her work of receiving lepers without homes or whoever needed to be looked after, at Titagarh, close to Calcutta. At first, the Sisters were in charge of the house. But they found it too difficult to deal with some of the cases, so Mother asked her Brothers to take over this home. They did so and till today run the institute very successfully, training the lepers to perform works or tasks they are able to do.

The patients had an occasion to show their mettle one night. One of the Brothers recalled, 'That night, there was some noise on the roof, where bags of rice had been stacked for protection against thieves. A group of men were busy pulling away the bags of rice. The patients climbed on the roof with sticks. They attacked the thieves, started hitting them. Some thieves escaped while others were cornered and beaten badly enough to teach them a lesson. The police were informed and an enquiry started.'

The story was publicized in the papers so that many people came to know of the wonderful work done at Titagarh Leprosy Home.

A Way to Prevent Abortions

At women's meetings Mother would thunder against abortion but she was also the person who helped unwed mothers the most in their difficulty.

As she was talking to a priest in a small parlour of the Mother House, two gentlemen came in. They introduced themselves as the father and uncle of a young lady. 'My daughter has become pregnant,' said the father. 'She cannot have the child in our house. In our community it would make it impossible to marry her. So she must be delivered elsewhere.'

'That is quite easy,' said Mother, 'she can go to one of our houses, the Sisters will take care of her until and after her delivery. Is there any love for the child?'

'Not at present,' answered the father.

'Yes, but it may come,' said Mother. 'If there is no love and the mother abandons the child, we shall give it in adoption. If there is love, the mother may call for the child after one or two years, as she likes. Now you may bring your daughter here and one of our Sisters will look after her.'

The two gentlemen went away visibly relieved. 'That happens often here,' said Mother. 'We have saved many children in this way.'

The Runaway

Mother Teresa was walking to Saint Mary's Church on the same street where she lived in Calcutta when she noticed a little boy sitting under a tree on the pavement. She stopped and talked to him and discovered that he was all alone. It was getting dark so she asked one of the Sisters to take him to the children's home nearby and give him a bath and a clean set of clothes. The next day, Mother inquired about him and was told that he had run away. She told this story of the boy who ran away to be with his mother:

'He was found but ran away again. Then I told one of the Sisters: "Please follow the child and see where he goes when he runs away." The child was found but ran away the third time. A Sister went out again and found him under a tree with his mother. She had put a small earthenware vessel on two stones and was cooking something she had picked out of a garbage heap. The Sister asked the child: "Why did you run away from the home?" The child said: "This is my home because this is where my mother is."

'His mother was there. That was home.'

A Prime Minister's Visit

After she had worked ten years in Calcutta, Mother went to open houses in several places in India. On one occasion Mother received a visitor—the most important man in the country then, Prime Minister Jawaharlal Nehru.

Later Mother told a friend:

'Mr Nehru came to see our house in Delhi. As I always do with visitors, I first took him to the chapel saying, "Let us first pay our respects to the Master of the house." I went in and knelt down in prayer. Nehru stayed at the door and made a gesture of respect. His friend Krishna Menon, who was accompanying him, went inside the chapel and looked at an inscription that was on the wall. He asked me what it meant.

'As we came out I asked, "Sir, shall I tell you what we do?" Nehru answered, "No, Mother, I know it; that is why I came." We went upstairs and Nehru met the children.'

Many years later, Mother's relations with Nehru's daughter, Indira Gandhi, then prime minister, were excellent.

Mother said, 'Mrs Gandhi phoned our Sisters in Delhi saying, "Sisters, we had a big party yesterday. There are plenty of vegetables remaining. You may have them for the children. Please send your van to collect them."

'That happened several times,' added Mother.

The Child, the Teacher

*M*other would sometimes repeat the following incident as an example of a child teaching his parents.

Supertick and Littletick were brothers aged eight and ten. They were as naughty as Dennis the Menace and their pranks earned them these nicknames by which they were known in the neighbourhood where they lived.

Supertick's birthday was approaching and his parents asked him what he would like for a gift and whom he would like to invite to his party. Unlike in other years, his reaction was different. He remained pensive and later that night at dinner he said, 'Give all the money you would spend on me for my birthday to Mother Teresa.' His parents were very surprised. They did not remember having spoken to their children about Mother Teresa and her work.

On the morning of his son's birthday, the father got ready early and before going to office, the whole family went to meet Mother. They handed an envelope containing the money to the birthday boy. He shyly shoved it into Mother's hands. She kissed him and gave him a 'return' present—her blessing and small medallions and cards addressed in her own handwriting to Supratik and his brother Ritwick—for these were their proper names.

The Courage to Give

Groups and individuals flocked to Mother Teresa and asked her how they could help her in her work among the poorest of the poor. Mother always told them that their families came first and so, before she directed them to work in any one of her homes, she would spend time talking to them about their families and neighbours.

'I want you to find the poor, right in your own home first. And begin love there. And find out about your next-door neighbours. Do you know who they are?'

She told them her own 'most extraordinary experience of love of one's neighbour' shown by a very poor Hindu family.

'A gentleman came to our house and said: "Mother Teresa, there is a family with eight children who have not eaten for sometime. Do something for them." So I took some rice and went there immediately. And I saw the children—their eyes shining with hunger. I don't know if you have ever seen hunger. It is a terrible thing—the look on the face of a hungry person—but I have seen it very often. The mother of that family took the rice from my hands and divided it in two. She took half of it and went out of the house. When she came back, I asked her: "Where did you go? What did you do?" And she gave me a very simple answer: "They are hungry also."

'What struck me was that she knew that the next-

door neighbours were hungry, too. And who were they?
A Muslim family. I was not surprised that she gave, but
I was very much surprised that she knew, because as a
rule when we are suffering, when we are in trouble, we
have no time for others. Yet this mother knew and had
the courage of her love to give.'

Divine Providence

One morning, Mother was sitting in the open courtyard of Mother House attending to the many visitors seeking her advice and help. She told them this story.

'Sometime ago, a man came to Mother House with a prescription. His only child was dying. The doctor had prescribed a medicine which was not available in India. I have permission from the government of India to get life-saving medicines which can come from anywhere. At that moment, a man came bringing a basket full of medicines which he had collected. Right on top was the medicine the man needed and just the right amount was there. If I had been somewhere else in the house and not there at that time, I wouldn't have seen it.

'There are millions of children dying in the world. See God's concern to get the medicine for that child. That is God's tenderness and love. That is loving trust—Divine Providence.'

Charity Begins Today

*M*other believed in immediate action. She was a doer, not a preacher. She would often say:

'Charity begins today. Today somebody is suffering, today somebody is in the street, today somebody is hungry. Our work is for today, yesterday has gone, tomorrow has not yet come. We see a need, we go to meet it; at least, we do something about it.

'A woman came with her child to me and said, "Mother, I went to two or three places to beg for food, for we have not eaten for three days but they told me that I was young and I should work and earn my living. No one gave me anything."

'I went to get some food for her, and by the time I returned, the baby in her arms had died of hunger.

'We will not have them tomorrow if we do not feed them today. So be concerned about what you can do today.'

Prizes for the Poor

One afternoon, Mother was talking to a group of visitors in the parlour of Mother House when she saw a small group of children accompanied by a middle-aged bespectacled lady standing in the doorway. 'Does Mother Teresa live here?' they asked in unison. When she saw them, she instinctively knew that these little visitors had come on a special mission. She excused herself and went to meet them.

After some time she returned to the parlour and told her visitors the reason for the interruption.

The children were students of a school in a suburb of Calcutta. The woman accompanying them was their headmistress. She told Mother that they had stood first and second in their respective classes and on the day before the Prize Distribution they asked her to give them money instead of prizes. The money was then put in an envelope. Their next demand was, 'Take us to Mother Teresa. We want to give this money to her poor people.'

Mother told her visitors, 'Now see, how wonderful it was that they did not use the money for themselves. Whenever I accept money or an award or anything, I always take it in the name of the poor whom they recognize in me. I think I am right because, after all, who am I? I am nothing. Because they see, they believe.'

A Media Star

A Jesuit priest who was Mother Teresa's spiritual adviser for many years wrote: 'The media helped Mother to become what she is and in the process made her a media star.'

Mother Teresa herself did not watch TV but whenever she appeared on the small screen, she was big news. On the subject of television and Mother, one of the Sisters retells a story that Mother had told her.

'A Brazilian man in a high position wrote to Mother Teresa that he had lost faith in God and in man, and he had given up his position and everything, even watching TV, and he only wanted to commit suicide. One day, as he was passing by a shop, his eyes suddenly fell on a TV, and there was a scene of Nirmal Hriday, the Home for the Dying in Calcutta. Mother and the Sisters were looking after the sick and the dying. He wrote to Mother that after seeing that scene he had knelt down and prayed for the first time after many years. Now he has decided to turn back to God and have faith in humanity because he saw that God still loves the world and he saw this on TV.'

Little Actions, Great Love

 $\mathcal{M}$ other Teresa knew that people were looking for ways and means to put their love into action, so she put forth their unasked question: 'How do we love?'

'Not in big things but in small things, with great love,' was Mother's answer.

She once illustrated what she had said with one of her own acts of love.

'In Melbourne, where we had gone to work, I met a man and I asked him if he would allow me to clean his house and wash his clothes. He said: "I'm alright." I said: "You will be more alright if you allow me to do these things."

'After I had finished, I saw a big beautiful lamp full of dust in the room. I asked him, "Don't you light this lamp?" and he replied, "For whom? For years nobody has come to see me. I do not need the lamp."

'I asked him, "Will you light the lamp if the Sisters come to see you?"

'He said, "Yes, if I hear a human voice, I will."

'So the Sisters started visiting him. After two years he sent me word: "Tell my friend that the light she has lighted in my life is still burning. It is still alight."

'See, that little act was something so beautiful. It is our little actions that can create much love.'

A Silver Jubilee Lunch

The Silver Jubilee of Nirmal Hriday, Mother's Home for the Dying, was celebrated on 22 August 1977. It was a very special occasion for Mother. That day, well-dressed ladies arrived in chauffeur-driven limousines. Mother had requested each of them to prepare and bring food for ten persons according to a fixed menu. They entered the home bearing trays and baskets of food and fruit. One lady came empty-handed and offered Mother some money. Mother said, 'I don't have a bag,' and asked her to give it to one of the Sisters. Later, Mother explained, 'I want the rich people to do the work themselves.'

Mother Teresa herself attended to every detail. She propped up the patients who could not sit up on their own and when she noticed that one patient could not swallow, she took an orange, peeled it and pressed the juice into his mouth.

No one was forgotten in the distribution and finally, when bags of nuts were about to be given, Mother, ever watchful, told the volunteers to keep the nuts for another time.

'They might suffer from indigestion if they eat any more; their stomachs are not accustomed to such large quantities of food.'

An Unusual Travelling Companion

$\mathcal{M}$other Teresa had received from Fatima, in Portugal, a beautiful statue of the Blessed Virgin Mary as she was depicted by the children to whom she appeared several times.

The devotion to Our Lady of Fatima had spread widely. In Calcutta a church was built and named in her honour.

Mother took the statue to several of her houses in India so that people might come and pray to the Mother of Jesus. She had received a free pass on the Indian Railways from the railway minister which specified: 'Free travel for Mother Teresa and a companion.'

Mother Teresa told this story to a friend, with a chuckle:

'Once on a journey, as I was seated with the statue next to me, a ticket examiner asked for my ticket. I showed him my pass. The man remarked, "There is no mention of free luggage, so you must pay for the statue that occupies a seat."

' "She is my companion," I replied, "she travels with me." The man objected: "But she does not talk."

' "I talk to her," I replied, "and she listens; and sometimes she talks to me. So I will not pay."

' "You must pay," he insisted.

' "How can I pay? I have no money. When I travel by

train I take no money, since I have a pass from the railway minister."

' "Alright," said the man, and he went away.'

As usual Mother had her way.

Professor of Love

Mother opened her first mission outside India in Venezuela. A rich family in Cocorote had given land to the Missionaries of Charity to build a home for orphaned children. When Mother Teresa visited South America, she went to thank the family. She noticed that their first-born child was 'terribly disabled.'

She asked the mother, 'What is his name?'

'Professor of Love,' replied the mother, 'because this child is teaching us the whole time how to express love in action.'

'There was a beautiful smile on the mother's face as she said these words,' said Mother.

Open Your Eyes

Mother Teresa's friends and followers were drawn to her from all walks of life and religions. Speaking to a group which she knew had never felt the pangs of hunger for food, but perhaps silently suffered the hunger for love, she told about this experience which had greatly moved her.

'None of us know what is the pain of hunger, but one day I learnt it from a little child. I picked up the child from the street. He was just six years old. I could see from his eyes that he was very, very hungry. I have seen that terrible hunger in many eyes. I gave him a piece of bread and instead of eating it as fast as possible, he started eating it crumb by crumb. I said to him: "Eat, eat the bread, you are hungry," and that little one looked at me and said: "I am afraid that the bread will be finished and I will be hungry again."

'That little one already knows the terrible pain of hunger which you and I may not know. That is why I say: Open your eyes and see, for there is hunger not only for a piece of bread; there is hunger for understanding love, for the word of God.'

An Answer to a Prayer

*I*n the early days of Mother Teresa's foundation, a man gave a donation of sixteen white cotton saris with red borders. She was thrilled and knew exactly what she was going to do with the gift. It was a part of Mother's routine to walk from Mother House to Shishu Bhavan, the children's home, two or three times a day where she prayed with the children and young girls and also fed and talked to them. Mother knew that the next day was a special occasion, a Feast Day, so in the evening, she and another Sister carried the saris to Shishu Bhavan. The girls were delighted to receive them and the saris were carefully stored away for the morrow.

The scene next morning was very different. The girls were crying their hearts out. Thieves had broken in during the night and among other things, had stolen the new saris. The news reached Mother House.

Mother came, and drawing the girls around her, she comforted them and asked them to pray that God may return the stolen saris to them. The crying stopped and they went down on their knees and prayed with Mother.

Though the tears had dried, a cloud of sadness hung over Shishu Bhavan as the hour approached for the big event. Just as the girls were getting ready, Mother received word that all the stolen items had been recovered by the police and were on their way to the home.

One of the boys, now a young man and a chef in a four-star hotel, remembers the incident and Mother's words: 'Everything starts with prayer. God always answers our prayer though we sometimes do not get what we asked for. God knows what is best for us.'

The boy told his foster aunt the story and added that though he was only seven or eight years old at the time, he had felt sad in the midst of the joy of the returned saris. The X-ray machine that had been recently donated was so badly damaged by the thieves that it could not be repaired. He remembered Mother telling the children what a wonderful machine it was because it could help so many poor, sick people.

The Sound of Singing

*I*t was one of the hottest summers in living memory when Mother, with a small band of Sisters, came to open a house at Lucknow, the capital of Uttar Pradesh. The summer temperatures here rise to over 40°C in the shade. But for Mother Teresa such considerations were incidental. She took them in her stride and never lost her earthy sense of humour.

She later wrote to a friend in Lucknow who was away at the time:

'You will be pleased to know that the heat in Lucknow has been really hot! So our Lucknow house was founded on Burning Love. It is good to burn with the heat of God outside since we don't burn with the heat of God in our hearts.'

The house was in an old English cemetery and knowing the apprehensions people have about cemeteries, Mother warned her friend that if she heard the sound of laughter and singing at night, she would know 'it is the Sisters singing.'

Sharing the Joy of Loving

Once Mother Teresa received a letter and some money just before she was leaving to give a talk and she shared the contents with her audience.

A child was going to take her First Communion. For a Catholic child, the preparation for, and reception of, the First Holy Communion is a very important event. The child wears new clothes and after the ceremony, a celebratory breakfast is often held. Relations and friends attend bearing small gifts.

The child told her parents, 'I don't want you to buy anything for me. I will take my First Communion in my school uniform, but give me the money you would have spent and I will send it to Mother Teresa.'

The father thought that if his child could do that, then he would give up something also. So he gave up drinking. The mother thought in the same way and gave up smoking. When the gift for Mother arrived from the child who lived very far away, it was from the whole family.

Mother said, 'They shared from so far. They shared the joy of loving. It was a beautiful sacrifice. At home, in the family, the child shared the joy of loving.'

Mother Teresa, an Air Hostess

It was very important that the Sisters working in far-flung countries around the world have Mother's presence among them from time to time. In India, Mother travelled on the cheapest railway ticket until she received a free pass for herself and a companion from the minister of railways. But international travel was expensive and it really hurt Mother to have to spend so much money on an airline ticket. Surely there must be a way out. Mother prayed.

The next time she had to go abroad, she went to the airlines office and asked if there was any work she could do on the plane that would earn her a free passage—as an air hostess, perhaps!

Mother's prayers were answered. In 1977 she was happy to say:

'The international air companies have started giving us free passage. We were already helped by the Indian domestic airlines but now the international companies also come to our help. Once, we were given six free tickets on an international flight and I sent six Sisters with one thousand pounds of luggage. The airport staff at first looked scared. They had never seen such a thing. The usual allowance is twenty kilos. But then the free pass did not specify any amount. It said: "Six Sisters and their luggage." So we sent blankets, medicines, foodstuff, all things needed to start working for the poor. Everything had to go.'

The thousand pounds of luggage were loaded on to the aircraft for no one would have dared to contradict Mother who ordered it for the sake of charity. And with her sense of humour she enjoyed telling the story.

Mother and Mahatma Gandhi

On 2 October 1976, Mother Teresa laid the foundation stone of the Institute of Gandhian Studies in Allahabad. She had agreed to accept because she hoped that all the people who were, and who would in the future be, involved in Mahatma Gandhi's work, would dedicate their lives 'to spread the gift of God that was given to Gandhiji.' When she was invited to speak, she asked the students and teachers to say a prayer with her, a prayer she felt that Mahatma Gandhi must have said often:

Make us worthy, Lord
To serve our fellow men throughout the world
Who live and die in poverty and hunger;
Give them through our hands this day their daily
*   bread*
And by understanding love, give peace and joy.

'Gandhiji loved his people as God loved him and he said: "He who serves the poor serves God." The one beautiful thing that strikes me most is his non-violence and also his comparing service to the poor with love for God. I understand Gandhiji's non-violence to be not only not using guns and bombs but first developing love and peace and compassion in our own homes. This spreads non-violence outside the home.'

Seeing a large number of young people in the gathering, Mother Teresa dedicated a special message to them:

'Young people today aim at one thing only, to give all or nothing. Gandhiji's non-violence is nothing but love for his people. I hope the young people will understand that sentiment of love of Gandhiji and, like him, surrender themselves to spread love and peace by the works of love that they do to each other.

'Let us bring the teaching of Gandhiji into our very home and make our homes and neighbourhood an abode of love, of peace, of joy. Joy to be fruitful has to be shared.'

Interlude in Rotterdam: 1

*M*other Teresa opened a new house in Rotterdam, Netherlands, in 1977. The Sisters had no difficulty in adapting to their new environment. One room was immediately converted into a very beautiful but simple chapel. Three vases of tulips adorned the altar. The bishop celebrated Mass in English and, after the service, was happy to have the chance to talk to Mother Teresa. He asked her many questions such as what was required of candidates wishing to join her Order.

'They should apply for the right reason, to serve Jesus in the poor. They should know something of our kind of life. They should possess sufficient health, a sound judgement, a good moral character.'

Then he asked her a personal question. He had heard that she slept for only three hours at night. The bishop was amazed and perhaps, had his doubts. He again asked Mother how she did it and why?

'I have to. The night is the only time when I can think of my Sisters and arrange the work.'

He then asked the oft-repeated question—after Mother Teresa, what and who?

Her answer was the same as always: 'They will have no trouble. God will find a more humble person, more obedient to Him, more faithful, someone smaller, with a deeper faith, and He will do greater things through her.'

Interlude in Rotterdam: 2

*N*ow that the bishop had broken the ice, he confided in Mother. He had to write an article for a paper on the future of the Catholic church. Would there be women priests? Would priests be permitted to marry? To the first question Mother said, 'Jesus did not make his mother a priest. If he did not make women priests, why should we?' And as for the future of the Church, Mother said, 'The future is not in our hands. We have no power over it. We can act only today.' She quoted a clause from the Constitution of the Missionaries of Charity:

'We will allow the good God to make plans for the future—for yesterday has gone, tomorrow has not yet come and we have only today to make Him known, loved and served.'

A Prayer Card for the President of India

Mother Teresa must have been one of the very few persons—if not the only one—who could meet successive presidents of India at New Delhi without any previous appointment. She just went to Rashtrapati Bhavan, the presidential residence, and sent up her name. She was received immediately.

What the president and she spoke about or what advice she gave, she did not reveal. On one special occasion, she did tell some friends about a public reception that was given to her in the capital before she left India to receive the Nobel Peace Prize. She did not dwell long on the reception but was excited about her meeting with President Neelam Sanjiva Reddy that same day.

'I went to Rashtrapati Bhavan to call on the president of India. When he met me, he pulled out of his pocket a card on which I had written the prayer of Newman: "Jesus shine through me" which we say daily in the chapel. I had given it to him when I had met him before and had told him to say it in times of difficulty.

'He told me, holding the card in his hand, "I say the prayer and it gives me consolation in times of stress and difficulty." '

Fruit of Forgiveness—Peace

Mother Teresa was neither fearful nor was she indecisive. If she felt that she could do something to alleviate human suffering, she and her Sisters would be there. She was amongst the first to arrive at scenes of devastation caused by earthquakes, floods and drought. She brought relief, spiritual and material, to families torn asunder by conflicts and wars. She gave solace to those who had lost their homes for no fault of their own. For her, the refugee camps around the world were 'like one big Calvary where Christ was crucified once more.'

'Help is needed,' she always said. 'But unless there is forgiveness, there will be no peace.' And forgiveness begins with personal attitudes.

She recounted one of her many experiences which had given her another insight into human nature.

'We have a home for the homeless in Melbourne and one of the men was very badly hurt by another. I thought it was a case for the police and sent for them. The policeman asked the gentleman the name of the person who had hit him but he wouldn't give the name. The policeman had to go away without doing anything. I asked the injured man why he hadn't told the police the truth. He looked at me and said: "His suffering is not going to lessen my suffering." '

An Indian by Choice

*I*t was possible to speak to Mother Teresa about anything and everything and not shock or surprise her. Lesser mortals might even have been indignant at some of the questions Mother Teresa was asked, but Mother, never. She answered with a smile even though she was often aware of the provocation.

In 1979, the year Mother Teresa won the Nobel Peace Prize, many organizations, governmental and nongovernmental, held meetings to congratulate her. In Calcutta, her own city, the West Bengal government convened an open-air civic reception in her honour. The chief minister presided. Television crews from several countries and hundreds of photographers and journalists were constantly 'shooting' the chief guest.

After the meeting, a journalist said: 'Mother, you must now consider yourself as a citizen of the world.' Mother answered: 'I am a citizen of India.'

Another media person took her up on her answer, 'Do you really consider yourself an Indian?'

The small sari-clad figure wrapped in an oversize navy blue cardigan replied, 'Yes, and I feel Indian to the most profound depths of my soul but there is a difference.' And addressing the Indian gentleman who had posed the question, she said: 'You are an Indian by accident (of birth); I am an Indian by choice.'

The Greatest Destroyer of Peace

*I*n 1994, Mother Teresa wrote to her co-workers in Calcutta that she had been invited to the National Breakfast held annually in Washington and enclosed a copy of her talk. Since Mother herself never wrote out her speeches for any occasion, big or small, the only way that she could have recaptured the text was through a recorded tape sent to her.

Before the meeting, Mother asked her friends to place a printed sheet on each chair. It was the Peace Prayer of Saint Francis of Assisi. When it was Mother's turn to speak, she invited her audience to take up the prayer sheets and pray together.

'It was beautiful to hear five thousand voices united in prayer to God. Then I spoke to them about the greatest destroyer of peace in the world today—abortion, because it is a war against the child, a direct killing of the innocent child, murder by the mother herself. And if we accept that a mother can kill even her own child, how can we tell other people not to kill each other?

'How do we persuade a woman not to have an abortion? As always, we must persuade her with love and we must remind ourselves that love means to be willing to give until it hurts.

'The father of that child, whoever he is, must also give until it hurts. By abortion, the mother does not learn to love, but kills her own child to solve her problems. And, by abortion, the father is told that he does not have to take any responsibility at all for the child he has brought into the world. That father is likely to put other women into the same trouble. So abortion just leads to more abortions.

'Any country that accepts abortion is not teaching its people to love, but to use violence to get what they want. This is why the greatest destroyer of love and peace is abortion.'

God's Greatest Gift

*M*other Teresa was talking to a group in the United States. She began by telling them that she had spoken to the First Lady about her strategy to fight abortion by adoption—by taking care of the mother and finding loving foster parents for her baby. Almost in the same breath Mother told them, 'I asked her to give us a house where we can help young women who want to give up their babies for adoption.'

She went on to tell them about 'something beautiful' that the Missionaries of Charity were doing: 'We have saved thousands of lives. We have sent word to the clinics, to the hospitals and police stations: "Please don't destroy the child; we will take the child." '

She talked about Shishu Bhavan, her home for homeless children in Calcutta, and looking at their serious faces, she smiled: 'Our house is full, full of children; and the people have a big joke. They say: "Mother Teresa is talking the whole time about family planning, but she herself is not practising it. Everyday she had more and more children!" ' Everyone was smiling.

'We always have someone to tell the mothers in trouble: "Come, we will take care of you, we will get a home for your child." And we have a tremendous demand from couples who cannot have a child. Jesus said: "Anyone who receives a child in my name, receives me."

'I can't tell you what the child has brought to these families that have no children. Think of the loneliness of these families! And the moment the child comes into their lives, they radiate joy.

'I can never forget the time when I gave a child to a family and after a few months I heard that the child had become very, very sick. I went to the family and told them: "Give me back that child. I'll take care of the sick child and I'll give you another healthy child." The father looked at me and said, "Mother, take my life rather than the child." '

Animal Lover

The Silver Jubilee of a high school at Sahebganga was being celebrated and Mother was present to preside over the main function.

News spread quickly that Mother Teresa was there and would make a speech. Soon a crowd of people came to hear her. The hall could not accommodate them, so they were told to go to the park where Mother would speak. Mother willingly did so. Later, she returned to the school for tea with the staff.

The priest who came daily to say Mass for the Sisters always brought his big Alsatian dog along, but the Superior would never allow it to enter the house. When Mother returned to the house she went to the reception room to meet the Sisters. During tea Father came in; the dog followed him and sneaked in. The Sister Superior got up to chase it out, but the dog rushed to Mother's feet. She exclaimed, 'What a nice dog!' and held it in her arms and kissed it. Mother as usual won the day and the dog remained close to her during tea.

As a result, from the next morning the big Alsatian was allowed into the house, because Mother had blessed it.

The Last Word

In Japan, as elsewhere in the world, Mother Teresa spoke about the vocation of hundreds of young women who left their homes and joined her Order. This thought may have been uppermost in Mr Hideki Izumi's mind when he asked her a question about her family.

Mr Izumi began by telling Mother that he had two daughters, one aged eight years and the other thirteen, and that he would be very unhappy if one of them entered religious life.

Mother said, 'A vocation is not the work of human hands. A vocation is between God and your daughters . . .' and added, 'If you have two, you must pray that God will call one of your daughters to belong to Him. That is the greatest gift of God to a family . . . if God calls your son or daughter to come to His service you are blessed.'

Knowing what was passing through the gentleman's mind, Mother smiled at him and said, 'God always hears my prayers.'

Mr Izumi exclaimed, 'Oh! That would be the destruction of my family!'

Mother continued smiling and gently teased him: 'You will be able to come to Calcutta then, to meet her!'

Mr Izumi was not amused and kept repeating that it would be the cause of great disunity in his family. He said, 'I find it hard to imagine a family that would be happy to have their daughter enter religious life,' and popped his question: 'I would like to know what kind of a family your own family was.'

Mother replied, 'I had a very happy family. And it was very difficult for my mother to give me, but she did. This is the sacrifice. Say, if your daughter gets married and goes away, you will have to give your daughter all the same. So, instead of giving her to somebody, you give her to God. This is the difference. We have in our Congregation thirty-five nationalities. We are over two thousand Sisters.'

With a twinkle in her loving blue eyes she had the last word, 'So, two thousand and one!'

Give Your Heart

Surrounded by, and working with, human suffering in its most acute form, Mother Teresa never worried about the wherewithal, but proceeded single-mindedly and serenely. She urged her listeners not to be satisfied with just giving money. 'Money is not enough. Money can be got. Give your heart to love and spread love everywhere you go.'

She remembered the 'very rich man' who had met her on the streets of Calcutta.

He asked, 'Are you Mother Teresa?'

Mother Teresa replied, 'Yes.'

'Please come or send somebody to my house. See, I am half blind and my wife is nearly mental. Our children have all gone abroad and we are dying of loneliness. We are longing for the sound of a human voice.'

'When the Sisters went there,' Mother said, 'they found that what he had said was true. They had everything but they were unwanted, unusable, so to say, unprofitable, and so they were dying of sheer loneliness.'

Love in Action

From time to time, Mother would write to her co-workers giving them news about the activities of the Missionaries of Charity and add a special message for them.

In one of her newsletters, she retold a story told by her Sisters working in Australia:

'There was a man on the street and nobody touched him. The Sisters picked him up, took him to the House of Compassion, our home. Here the Sisters loved and cared for him. One day, after sixteen long years, he said: "Sister, I am going home and I will never, never drink again. The way you loved and cared for me, I suddenly realize that God loves me."

'He went home but returned with his first salary. "Sister," he said, "Here is my first salary. Do to others what you did to me."

'That man put God's love in action.'

Mother Wants Me

To volunteers in rich countries, Mother Teresa would speak of another kind of poverty—poverty of the spirit. She said, 'There is homelessness not only of people sleeping in the streets of Calcutta, Rome and many other places including San Francisco, where it is said that about five thousand people sleep in the streets at night. It's not only that kind of homelessness, but the homelessness of being rejected, being unwanted, unloved and uncared for. We live in a throw-away society. And we have so many people who have been thrown away.

'I'll never forget a little child who came knocking on our door around midnight, crying at the top of his voice and saying: "I went to my father, my father didn't want me. I went to my mother, my mother didn't want me. Do you want me?"

'Naturally I wanted him very much, for that little one was so hurt.'

A Sword of Honour

*M*other Teresa related to her listeners how the work of her mission was received in the Middle East.

'We work in various Muslim countries. In Yemen we have three places. The government has given us a whole mountain for the rehabilitation of lepers and has built the necessary constructions. It is very difficult work but it is wonderful that they understand Christian love by observing the dedication of the Sisters. The prime minister was very grateful for the good work of the Sisters and as a token of gratitude he presented me with a Sword of Honour, their highest decoration.

'He also asked me to bring our Sisters to open a school for the girls of the upper class. I told him we worked only for the very poor and suffering and accepted no payment. As he might not understand what our vow is, I said, "We have given our word to God; when you give your word you must keep it. Is that not so?" "Yes," he replied, "if you give your word, you must keep it."

'We have also established a home for the dying. The governor of Hodeidah wrote to Rome and said, "The presence of the Sisters has lit a new light in the lives of our people." '

Deeds, Not Words

The criticism that Mother Teresa faced, especially in non-Christian countries, was that the ultimate goal of her work was to proselytize. The Hindu priests at a Kali temple were unhappy when Mother and the Sisters began their work at Nirmal Hriday in Kalighat close to the temple. Then something happened that brought about a complete change of heart.

Mother heard that one of the priests of the temple was dying of an infectious disease and nobody would touch him. She collected his emaciated body in her arms and brought him to her home.

The local people asked her to stay. A Hindu priest of the temple said to her with folded hands, 'For thirty years I have worshipped the goddess Kali in stone, but today the goddess Mother stands before me alive.'

The Universal Language

Mother Teresa accepted the invitation of the bishop of Venezuela to come and see the plight of a landless community. She decided to open her first mission outside India in Cocorote, Venezuela in 1965. The Sisters opened an atlas to locate the place. Mother, observing them with amusement, said, 'If there are poor people on the moon, we will go there.' She knew that the cosmonauts had reached it already.

She chose four Indian Sisters. They were thrilled but felt nervous and asked, 'How will we manage in a new country of which we know neither the language nor the customs?'

Mother allayed their fears and doubts. She said, 'Fear not, little ones. You speak the language all men understand, the language of charity.'

Where Angels Fear to Tread

Mother Teresa had three houses in Rome but she had set her heart on a house within the walls of the Vatican. She told Pope John Paul II about her desire and on a subsequent visit, she broached the subject again. At her request, he gave orders that a suitable place be found for Mother. It is said that he made tentative inquiries about the plan of the house. He knew that on Mother's next visit she would remind him again. So, before her fourth visit in 1988, he made sure that he had the key of the new building to give her even before she could ask.

With a twinkle in her eyes, Mother Teresa would tell this story of the triumphal entry of the poor into the Vatican.

'In the Vatican, it is so beautiful, we have seventy ladies staying there and a soup kitchen for the men. It is a wonderful gift to Saint Peter. All these years, nobody could go here or there without being stopped by the police and the guards, but now our poor people can go wherever they want freely, without any ticket.

'When we were about to get into the Vatican, I went to the Holy Father to get the plan signed for the Casa Dono di Maria. Otherwise, nobody would accept it, not even the cardinals. They would say to me: "The Vatican! What, coming here?" '

When they actually said this to Mother, she showed them the proof—the plan signed by the Pope.

Mother was happy. She said, 'It has been a real good thing to have our home there,' and she added with child-like simplicity, 'The Holy Father sends us food whenever he can.'

She could not resist telling her listeners, 'Do you know who gave the very first gift to the Vatican home? The children of London. It was £123 from children aged eight and nine years.'

'Your Job Qualifications, Mother?'

People had warned Mother Teresa that it would not be easy to set up a house in Ethiopia but she was undaunted. They told her that many organizations had not been allowed to work. But the starving children of that country pulled at her heartstrings. 'We must go,' she told her Sisters.

Mother Teresa arrived in Addis Ababa with her Sisters, gauged the situation for herself and then purposefully pursued ways and means to obtain an audience with the emperor. She made friends with a close relative of Emperor Haile Selassie, but the minister in the Imperial Court who was the screening authority intercepted Mother Teresa. He began his inquisition by asking her what she wanted from the government.

'Nothing,' she replied, a trifle surprised, 'I have come to offer my Sisters to work among the poor suffering people.'

He told her that a great famine had overtaken the country and thousands of men, women and children were dying of malnutrition. 'What will your Sisters do?' he asked.

Mother replied, 'We give wholehearted free service to the poorest of the poor.'

Somewhat baffled by her answer, the minister demanded, 'What qualifications do you have?'

Mother, without a moment's hesitation, said, 'We bring love and compassion to the people.'

The minister could not contain himself any longer and asked her bluntly, 'Do you preach to the people and try to convert them?'

Mother looked him in the eyes and gave him her beatific smile: 'Our works of love reveal to the suffering poor the love of God for them.'

The minister was dumbfounded. He granted Mother an audience with Emperor Selassie. When she was ushered into his presence, the emperor said, 'I have heard about your good work. I am happy to allow your Sisters to come to Ethiopia.'

It was 1973. Mother Teresa opened her first home in Ethiopia. A year later, Selassie was deposed. The Sisters stayed on.

The Beggar's Mite

The demands on Mother Teresa's time were legion—demands were made by individuals and institutions, especially during the last two decades of her life. Her presence at any occasion, whether cutting ribbons or lighting lamps at the inauguration of baby shows and seminars, sports meets and convocations, was always a big draw and a feather in the cap of the organizers.

In 1980, Mother was asked to speak at the convocation at Kurukshetra University. As was her way, she prayed aloud that all the young men and women who had graduated would carry 'not just a piece of paper with them but love, peace and joy.'

She said, 'Don't forget your brothers and sisters. You have received not to keep, but to share. And not to give from your abundance, but to give until it hurts. It is not how much you give, but with how much love you give it.'

From her precious fund of real-life stories, Mother told them one of her most moving experiences.

'In Calcutta, a beggar came to me and said, "Mother Teresa, everybody is giving you something. I also want to give you something. I have just this ten-paise coin, will you accept it?" '

Mother was in a dilemma. She said, 'I knew if I accepted the money, he would go hungry and if I did not, he would be hurt, so I put out my hand and took his gift.'

For Mother Teresa the beggar's mite was greater than the 'Oslo gift'—the Nobel Prize—because she said, 'He gave all that he had,' and she saw 'the joy of giving in his face.'

A London Cabby's Contribution

The Central Committee of co-workers in the United Kingdom was holding a meeting at Brompton Oratory Parish Hall in London. The Honorary Treasurer who lived outside London arrived at Waterloo station and hailed a taxi to take him to the venue. He asked the driver to hurry as he had to be at the Brompton Oratory by 10 a.m. It was a Wednesday morning and the driver was a little surprised. 'Sir, I am accustomed to rushing people to church on Sundays but this is the first time I have been asked to get someone to church on time on a Wednesday.' he said.

The gentleman explained that he was not going to church but to a meeting in aid of a charity. The driver asked politely what charity he was associated with.

'It is the charity of Mother Teresa and her Sisters,' said the passenger.

When the taxi arrived at its destination, the driver refused to accept the fare. 'Please put it in the collection,' he said.

As soon as the treasurer entered the Parish Hall, he told the delegates his experience and put the fare which had amounted to one pound and thirty pence in the collection box.

At Lourdes

The treasurer's story at Brompton Oratory set the mood for the meeting and prompted other members who were present to relate acts of love performed by children, individuals and groups, the rich and the poor. In all cases anonymity was the key note.

A delegate spoke of his experience. He had gone on a pilgrimage to Lourdes and had offered a 'big' candle at the grotto of Our Lady of Lourdes. In the evening, he was sitting with the other pilgrims when a man came up to him and said, 'Don't you work for Mother Teresa?' and before he could reply, he gave him a cheque for £3500.

The delegate handed the cheque to the treasurer and was told that it was the exact amount that was required to pay a bill for a shipment of food to Mother Teresa.

'Next time I go to Lourdes, I shall offer Our Lady an even bigger candle,' he concluded.

One of Mother's Little Wonders

Desmond Doig was one of the first journalists to write about Mother Teresa. He had worked with Mother for over two decades in Calcutta.

The writing of the book began with a prayer in the chapel on an evening when the electric power supply had failed, resulting in a candle-lit service. Mother Teresa insisted that the book should be about her work and her people only and so out of the several excellent titles Doig had in mind, he chose the most straightforward one: *Mother Teresa: Her People and Her Work.*

Doig, in his research for material for the book, had to follow Mother and her Sisters from early morning in the hot summer months but there were some unexpected bonuses.

Summer gave way to the monsoon and Doig sat down to write the book. A cool breeze blew through the open window of his apartment. He had finished writing the first page when he remembered an appointment with Father Henry, an important person in the spiritual lives of the Missionaries of Charity. He left his papers and rushed to meet him. By the time he got home it was pouring with rain. The first page of the book, which he had written before rushing out, had been blown out of the window. A search was started but there was no trace of the missing page of the manuscript. He sat down to the difficult task of starting all over again when the doorbell rang. It was the doorman with the missing page in his hand. It was bone dry. He had picked it up as it wafted toward him. Doig thought that this was just one of Mother's little wonders.

A Transformation

One morning, a well-known photographer went to Nirmal Hriday. His job was to take photographs for a book on the work that Mother Teresa and her Sisters were doing. Here he suddenly put aside his camera and sat down beside an old and wizened woman who was weeping. The woman looked intently into his face and asked him, 'Is it you, my son?'

Not wishing to disappoint the woman he replied spontaneously, 'Yes, mother, it is I.'

The woman said, 'I thought you would never come.'

'Now I am here. Don't worry anymore,' he reassured her.

The old lady drew her newly-found son to her and kissed him. 'God bless you, my son,' she said, 'now I can die happy.'

In the car on the way back, the photographer could not wait to tell Mother Teresa about the transformation that had taken place within him. He said to her, 'I did not believe in God but today I do.'

A Mystical Partnership

In Minneapolis, a woman, suffering continuous convulsions due to cerebral palsy came to meet Mother Teresa and asked her, 'What can people like me do for others?'

Mother told her, 'You can do the most. You can do more than any of us because your suffering is united with the suffering of Christ on the Cross and it brings strength to all of us. There is a tremendous strength that is growing in the world through this continual sharing, praying together and working together.'

Sick and crippled people often feel that they are useless; that they are a burden to society; that they cannot do anything to share the work. Mother thought and prayed and offered a two-way solution. She asked her active co-workers to 'adopt a Brother or a Sister sick co-worker' and involve him or her in the work. This mystical partnership proved to be a source of great strength to both. They called each other their 'second self'.

Mother adopted a second self in Belgium and each time she had something special or something difficult to do, she would say, 'It is she behind me that gives me all the strength and courage to do what I am doing. As my second self, she does the most difficult part of the work for me.'

During a particularly difficult time for Mother, her second suffering self who was about to undergo surgery for the seventeenth time said to her, 'I am sure you are going to have a heavy time with all the walking and working and talking. I know this from the pain I have in my spine.'

At the UN

Mother received a glorious reception at the United Nations Organisation in New York on the occasion of its fortieth anniversary celebrations.

In the main hall before a select assembly of diplomats, politicians and industrialists from all over the world, the premiere of the film, *Mother Teresa,* had been shown. At the end of the film as Mother was going to the rostrum she received a standing ovation from the assembly. Then the Secretary General of the UN told the audience: 'I present to you the most powerful woman in the world.' Those words are history.

What was Mother's reaction?

'It was wonderful in New York,' she told a priest, 'I made them pray in the hall where they had never prayed before. I told them: 'This beautiful organization was started forty years ago to ensure peace in the world. There has been no peace. Let us pray to the Only One who can ensure peace in the world. I had friends distribute slips with the Prayer for Peace of Saint Francis of Assisi. And so I led the congregation in praying to the one true God. Is that not wonderful?'

It was a repeat performance: she had done the same in Oslo in 1979 when receiving the Nobel Peace Prize.

Who Is a Communist?

When she was asked to speak at the fortieth anniversary celebrations of the United Nations, Mother summed up her thoughts and ideas on prayer, peace, love and joy. She commented: 'God loves us and He wants us to love one another as He loves each one of us. He has created us for that one reason—to love and be loved, no other reason. We are not just a number in the world, we are a child of God.

'Last time I went to China, they asked me, "What is a communist to you?" I said: "A child of God, my brother, my sister." And exactly that is what you and I are meant to be, brothers and sisters. If we have the joy of seeing God in each other, we will love one another. That's why no colour, no religion, no nationality should come between us for we are all the children of the same loving hand of God.'

A Personal Remembrance

Mother Teresa was reluctant to speak about herself or her family but she wanted to impress upon her co-workers that for those of them who were married, their husbands and children came first, and the example of her own mother was to her the best way she could inspire them.

'My own mother used to be very busy the whole day,' she said, 'but as soon as the evening came, she used to move very fast to get ready to meet my father. At that time, we didn't understand and we used to smile at each other and laugh and tease her. But now I realize what a tremendous, delicate love she had for him. It didn't matter what happened in the day, she was always ready with a smile to meet him.'

Mother was well aware of how the changing times had affected family life.

'Today we have no time. The father and the mother are so busy that when the children come home from school there is no one to love them, to smile at them. If you are not there, how will your love for one another grow?'

Love Begins at Home

Mother Teresa was surprised to see the increasing numbers of drug addicts among young boys and girls from rich as well as poor families and she tried to find out why this was so. She visited homes and rehabilitation centres and she found the answer.

'When they come home there is no one in the family there to receive them. Our children depend on us for everything—their health, their nutrition, their security, their coming to know and love God. For all this they come to us with trust, hope and expectation.'

The weakening of family bonds was at the root of the problem. 'Love the poor,' she said, 'but first of all love the members of your own family.' She shared her experience in London to bring home her message:

'One night I was walking down the streets with the Sisters. I found a young boy with long hair sitting in the street with others. And I said to him: "Why are you here? You shouldn't be here. You should be home with your parents." And then he said to me: "Mother, so often I tried to go home. My mother doesn't want me. Each time I go home she pushes me out because she can't bear my long hair."

'I gave him some soup and sandwiches and we passed on. On our way back, we found him lying flat on the ground. He had overdosed himself with drugs. We had to take him to the hospital. And I couldn't help thinking that maybe his mother was occupied with this thing and with that thing. But there was her own child, unwanted, unloved, just thrown away.

'I could not help but reflect: here was a child hungry for home, and his mother had no time for him. This is great poverty. This is where you and I must make this world a better world.'

Out of Love For Each Other

The shining example of two people in love with each other was close to Mother's heart and she would relate this story often to young audiences.

'In 1982, a young man and woman came to our house in Calcutta. They had heard that we cook for seven thousand people everyday and so they gave me a big amount of money to help feed the people.

'I asked them, "Where did you get so much money?"

'They answered, "Before our marriage, we decided that we were not going to have a wedding feast or buy any wedding clothes. And we decided to give that money to feed the poor."

'I was puzzled because in India marriage is a big thing. To have the courage to do what they had done was something extraordinary. So I asked them another question: "But why did you do that?" They answered, "Out of love for each other. We wanted to give each other something special, something beautiful and we gave this tender love in sacrifice."

'It's wonderful to think there is such tender love. I always pray: "Dear God, give the young people the grace and strength that on the day of their marriage they can give to each other a pure heart, a virgin heart, a virgin body which is the greatest gift of love for each other." '

'Give It Up'

A woman from Rajasthan came to me,' said Mother, 'and with tears she complained, "I have a child who is three years old but cannot speak."

'I asked the woman, "Is there anything you like very much that you could give up?" She answered, "Yes, betel-nut; I chew betel-nut the whole day."

' "Well," I told her, "give up betel-nut chewing. Offer it as a sacrifice to God. You ask for a big favour, give something in exchange." '

Mother said that the sacrifice of the lady from Rajasthan bore fruit. She returned to thank Mother and said, 'Now the child can speak.'

Manna from Heaven

At Shishu Bhavan in Calcutta hundreds of people are fed everyday. Mother Teresa recalls that one day a Sister came running to her and said that there was no more rice and asked what they should tell the people. Mother was a little anxious because such a situation had never occurred before. The next morning at nine o'clock, Mother was informed that a truck loaded with hundreds of quarter-pound loaves of bread was waiting at the gate. What should be done? That knowing expression lighted up her face and she hurried down the stairs, calling, 'Open the gates, of course.'

Children in government primary schools in Calcutta are provided with a midday tiffin which is usually bread. The government, for some unknown reason, had suddenly declared that the schools should be closed for two days.

Mother continued to tell the story animatedly: 'Nobody knew why, and so the bread for the midday tiffin was brought to Shishu Bhavan, and for two days our poor people ate bread and bread and more bread! I know why God closed the schools.'

Mother's deduction was simple. 'God wanted our people to know that they were more important than the grass and the birds and the flowers of the fields; that they were special to Him, that He cared for them.'

Mother Teresa
in the White House

President Reagan and his wife spent an hour with Mother Teresa in the White House. As soon as reporters could get hold of the president, they asked him what he had said to Mother.

The president answered, 'When you are with Mother Teresa, you listen.'

Hungry For God

Mother Teresa was invited to address the World Congress for the Pastoral Care of Tourism in the Vatican in 1984. In her address she asked: 'Why are people going around in circles? Is it just to see the scenery? There is not much point in that. There is something more. There is a great hunger for God in the world today. Travel is one way of showing that hunger.

'Why do people come to India? Because they believe that in India we have a lot of spirituality and this they want to find. Among them are hundreds of young people and from among them, thank God, many are now coming to our houses and are working with us. In Calcutta, they work in the Home for the Dying. Many are completely lost and so it is very important that they are guided.

'I remember some time ago, a young girl came from a university in Paris. She had told her parents that before she appeared for her final examination, she wanted to go to Mother Teresa and work with her. She came to Calcutta to see me. She looked very tired. Her eyes were not smiling. I suggested that she come to the chapel and pray with the Sisters. She regularly visited the Home for the Dying. After ten or twelve visits, she came and threw her arms around me and said: "Mother Teresa, I have found Jesus."

'I asked her: "Where did you find Jesus?"

' "In the Home for the Dying," she replied.

' "And what did you do after you found Jesus?" I asked.

' "I went to confession and Holy Communion after fifteen years."

' "What else did you do?" I asked again.

' "I sent a telegram to my parents to tell them that I have found Jesus."

'She was full of joy and smiles.'

A Buddhist Lady's Gift

A Buddhist lady from Nepal died leaving her property to Mother Teresa whom she had never met. It was a house with a large garden along the main road leading from the plains to Darjeeling in the Himalayas. It was situated near the small town of Tindheria. The bishop of Darjeeling told Mother about the legacy when she came to visit her houses there, but Mother said she would not accept it as she already had four houses in his small diocese.

The bishop pleaded that it was a nice place for children. It had a large playground, the pure air of the hills and a pleasant climate. Mother would not agree.

Then the bishop found the right approach. He said, 'Mother, there is no church and no place for prayer on this road from the plains to Kurseong, fifty kilometres away. If you open a house of the Missionaries of Charity, there will be a chapel where Jesus will be worshipped and people will come for Holy Mass and the sacraments.' This argument convinced Mother. 'I will take it,' she said.

After opening this new house Mother told the Sisters to bring the babies and young children from Darjeeling which is very cold in the winter, being at 6000 feet to Tindheria at 1500 feet.

Mother Teresa Has No Sugar

Those who have had the good fortune to meet Mother Teresa can never forget her smile. As she grew older and her face more wrinkled, every crease added to her loving smile. Children had a very special place in her heart and their little offerings were to her bigger than the biggest donation she had ever received.

Once, there was a sugar shortage in Calcutta and the Sisters came in relays from Shishu Bhavan to Mother, each one saying that there was no sugar for the children. In their preoccupation with the sugar crisis no one, except Mother, noticed that a four-year-old boy was standing in front of her and looking up into her face. She put her arms around the child and said, 'Mother Teresa has no sugar for her children.'

The boy went home and told his parents: 'I will not eat sugar for three days. I will give my sugar to Mother Teresa.'

A few days later, the boy led his parents to Mother House and in lisping syllables asked to see Mother. As soon as he saw her coming, he held out the bottle of sugar that he was firmly clutching in his two hands.

Mother repeated this story many times with great feeling and each time she would say, 'That little boy who could hardly pronounce my name loved with great love and that little one taught me that it is not how much we give, but how much love we put in that giving.'

Power of Prayer

Shishu Bhavan was a hive of activity as on any other morning. Sisters in aprons leaned over the cribs attending to the infants and children as if they were their very own. One Sister picked up a very sick baby in her arms. There seemed little hope that he would live through the day. Mother Teresa's words rang in the Sister's ears: 'A dying child must be loved and comforted. No one must die alone and uncared for.'

Mother Teresa was on her way elsewhere, when she told the driver to make a detour to the children's home. As soon as the Sister saw her entering, she ran to her with the baby. Mother Teresa took the infant in her arms and quietly said the Lord's Prayer:

Our Father who art in heaven, hallowed be thy name,
Thy kingdom come, thy will be done
On earth as it is in heaven.
Give us this day our daily bread,
And forgive us our trespasses
As we forgive them that trespass against us,
And lead us not into temptation
But deliver us from evil.

Mother Teresa handed the infant to the Sister and went about her business.

Next day, the volunteers entered anxiously, expecting to find another occupant in the cot. They saw the same baby but it was no longer critically sick.

One of the senior Sisters quietly commented, 'Such things happen here frequently.'

I Love You, God

After a long and lively interview with Mother Teresa, Mr Kato, a Japanese journalist, admitted, 'I still have trouble believing in God's love. What can you do with someone like me?'

Mother said: 'What you have to do is go down on your knees and pray:

> *My God, I believe in you.*
> *My God, I love you.*
> *My God, I trust you.*
> *I am sorry.*

'Then do some small things with great love. Help somebody. Maybe just smile. Is there a person who has hurt you? You go and forgive that person. Is there some bitterness? Go and say it is forgiven. And you will find Him. God cannot be found when we are unforgiving.

'Look at this flower. It is so beautiful. Can you make it or can I? Only He can. See the colours. This is the presence of God. Everyone here, each one has something beautiful. Take your body, it is so beautiful, so pure. Why? He has made it.

'Life? No one can give it but God. You can find Him in you. You will find that He was there all the time. He is in your heart, only you have covered Him up.'

Pointing to the instrument on the table, Mother continued, 'It is like this tape recorder. You don't see what is inside, but it is a beautiful tape recorder. God is inside your heart, but He is covered up, and you must believe.

'How do you believe? Say often during the day: "My God in my heart, I believe in your faithful love for me. I love you." Can you remember that? Can you write that? God loves me.'

Mother gave Mr Kato a card with the drawing of a child at rest in the Hand of God. Writing his name on it, Mother continued, 'You are that little child in the Hand of God. YOU.' She quoted from the Holy Bible: 'I will never forget you. I have carved you in the palm of my hand. I have called you by your name. You are mine. You are precious to me. I love you.' (Isaiah)

Mr Kato said, 'I understand that this child is me but I don't know if this is God's Hand or not!'

Mother replied, 'Do you find it difficult to believe that? Well, there is no need to believe. It is like that. Two and two make four. You don't have to believe. God is. There is nothing more to say than that.'

Mother and the Molecular Biologist

The impact of Mother Teresa's simple messages is very great and this has been witnessed time and again with audiences from the most sophisticated to her own poorest of the poor.

People in Canada still remember her appearance in a television programme with two well-known French scientists. She sat with her head bowed in prayer while the famous French molecular biologist and Nobel Prize winner animatedly spoke about how the destiny of man is inexorably locked up in his genes. When pressed by the compère for her views, she raised her head and remarked, 'I believe in love and compassion.'

Her intervention, reinforcing the other scientist's powerful Christian testimony, was somehow decisive and the Nobel laureate was afterwards heard saying that a little more of the same treatment and his sound atheistic position might be jeopardized.

Love and Forgive

With people who believe in an afterlife, Mother Teresa was acutely conscious of the importance of the last moments preceding death. She said that she had started Nirmal Hriday especially to help the poor people picked off the street to die a decent and holy death. And towards this end she would do whatever she could.

A woman left to die on a garbage heap was brought into the home. She was burning up with fever and kept repeating, 'It is my son who did this to me, my own son.' Mother related her experience as she sat holding the woman in her arms:

'We know that if we really want to love, we must learn to forgive. Reconciliation begins first, not with others but with ourselves. This woman was so hurt that her own child didn't want her; her son whom she had borne. She had given him love and care and now he had no use for her because she could no longer work and had become a burden to him. I begged her to forgive her son, to be a mother to her son. The woman could not get herself to forgive him for that indignity but after a long time she whispered in her last breath, "I forgive him my God, I forgive him." She was not concerned that she was dying. What had broken her heart was that her son did not want her. This is something you and I can understand.

'God will never do these things to us. Even if we com-

mit the greatest sin, we have only to say: "I'm sorry."
This is the greatness of the mercy of God, the tenderness
of God's love. It's wonderful. This is the love we must
learn.'

A Silent Sacrifice

In 1928 Mother Teresa came to Calcutta as a novice of the Institute of the Blessed Virgin Mary, better known as the Loreto Order. She was eighteen years old. The Loreto nuns are a teaching Order and Mother taught Geography and, later, was principal of Saint Mary's School in Calcutta. Many years later, one evening at recreation with the Missionaries of Charity, Mother was in a reminiscent mood and told the Sisters about her Loreto days.

One of Mother's duties was to accompany the children on their weekly walks. They lined up in pairs and called the formation a crocodile. Mother brought up the rear and partnered the naughtiest girl in the group, who was clutching a coin in her hand. The crocodile reached the Mall. The girl kept looking into the shop windows and repeating, 'I want to buy this, I want to buy that.'

Soon after, they passed a blind man who sat with his hand outstretched. Mother noticed that the girl had fallen silent and wondered why. She realized that the coin in the girl's hand had been quietly transferred to the blind beggar.

After telling the story, Mother would say, 'God gave her the joy and the courage to give the coin without a word, without a thank you, without drawing attention to herself.'

A Party For Two Thousand

An old friend came to see Mother as she was going out. 'You must come,' said Mother to her friend. 'It will be wonderful. We are having a big party for two thousand poor children of the slums. First there will be a show, then tea. I got some big business people to organize it and provide the transport to Tollygunge Club. I told them, "Ask your wives and daughters to come and distribute the tea packets to the children after the show, not your servants."

After this eventful party Mother said, 'It went off so well. The children were so happy, they had never enjoyed themselves so much. I saw some children patting the grass and they asked me, "What makes it grow so strong?" They had never seen such beautiful grass.

'I saw some children eating only one sweet from the tea packets they received. They said, "We have brothers and sisters at home and we want to share with them." Isn't that lovely, that charity among poor children?'

'Give Me Your Hands'

*M*embers of a well-known social service club came to give a donation to Mother Teresa. She knew they were some of the leading businessmen of the city and had brought a handsome donation. But it was not always easy to satisfy Mother. She reminded her co-workers that she did not want the work 'to become a business, but to remain a work of love.' The sacrifice of a missed meal given to the hungry was dearer to her than a millionaire's cheque. Thanking the members of the club in all humility, she said, 'I would like more people to give their hands to serve and their hearts to love.'

She then told them the story of a man who gave her a big donation but was not happy about it. He said, 'This is something outside of me. I want to give something of me.'

So he came regularly to the Home for the Dying in Kalighat and talked to the sick and the dying. He bathed and dressed them, manicured their nails, shaved their beards and combed their hair.

It is this other part of giving which Mother said 'is the harder part.'

Giving and Receiving

No letter box is big enough to receive all the mail that the postman sometimes brings to the headquarters of the Missionaries of Charity in Calcutta, so Mother Teresa decided to have a narrow rectangular opening made in the painted brown door at the entrance. The letters are collected in baskets and taken to the small office room on the first floor. Mother Teresa used to read all the letters addressed to her, and tried to reply to them herself, often in her own hand.

On one occasion, as she opened an envelope, three five-dollar bills fell out along with a note by a man who had been bedridden for twenty years. The only part of his body that he could move was his right hand, and his only companions were cigarettes which he enjoyed smoking now and again. The note read: 'I did not smoke for one week, and I send you this money.'

Mother was deeply touched. 'It must have been a terrible sacrifice for him. But see how beautiful it is, see how he shared. And with that money,' she said, 'I bought bread and I gave it to those who are hungry, with a joy on both sides. He was giving and the poor were receiving.'

Spiritual Poverty

Mother was visiting Japan and, as usual, nothing escaped her observant blue eyes. While being driven to the place where she was to speak to a Japanese audience, she saw a man under the influence of alcohol lying by the roadside. She took the opportunity at the meeting to comment on what she had seen: 'You are a rich nation but on one of your streets I saw a man lying drunk, and no one picked him up or was bothered about him. No one tried to restore to him his human dignity, to bring back to his senses that he had a brother, and was a child of God.'

Mother Teresa's Business Card

No one returned empty-handed from Mother Teresa. She would press a medal of the Virgin Mary into the palm of their hands, or a piece of paper with a prayer which she said, or a quotation from the Holy Bible. These she would autograph if asked to do so, no matter how pressed she was for time.

The pile of business cards handed to Mother Teresa in return, if placed one on top of the other, would have reached heaven! But Mother herself had no 'business' card and it did not cross her mind until one day, a businessman who met her briefly and wanted to contact her again, asked, 'Mother, may I have your business card?' Mother delved into the cloth bag with wooden handles that she carried when travelling and handed him a prayer card. He looked at it and asked again, 'Mother, don't you have a business card?'

Mother thought about the gentleman's question and late one night, she wrote out her own 'business' card in five lines:

> The fruit of SILENCE is Prayer
> The fruit of PRAYER is Faith
> The fruit of FAITH is Love
> The fruit of LOVE is Service
> The fruit of SERVICE is Peace
> —Mother Teresa

There was no address or telephone number!

When these omissions were brought to her attention, Mother said that she did not think it was important. 'This is very good "business"! It makes people think. Sometimes they ask me to explain it. But you see, everything begins with prayer that is born in the silence of our hearts. Among yourselves you can share your own experience of your need to pray, and how you found prayer, and what the fruit of prayer has been in your own lives.'

The Mystery of God

People who came to see Mother Teresa did not always have to spell out their problem or ask a question. She often perceived it.

At the Home for the Dying, a group of intellectuals were waiting for her. As if she could read their minds, she said, 'Why these people and not me? Why is that person picked up from the drain here, why not me? That is a mystery. Nobody can give the answer.

'Where there is a mystery, there must be faith. Faith you cannot change, no matter how you look at it. Either you have it, or you don't.'

Mother's faith was fathomless. She said, 'Our expanding knowledge does not dim our faith, it only shows the size of God's creation. Often we cannot understand. In the life of Saint Augustine there is a beautiful example.

'Saint Augustine was struggling to understand God, and the magnitude of God's creation. His human mind could not grasp it. He was searching everywhere when he came upon a small boy who was trying to put the ocean into a hole in the ground. Saint Augustine asked him what he was doing.

'The boy said, "I am trying to pour the ocean into this hole."

'Saint Augustine told him that it was impossible.

'Then the child, who, in truth, was an angel, said, "It is still easier to put the ocean into this hole than for you to understand the mystery of God." '

A Temporary Truce

$\mathcal{M}$other Teresa, the messenger of peace, would speak on the subject whenever she got a chance. She often exhorted her listeners, 'Let us not use bombs and guns to overcome the world. Let us radiate the peace of God and extinguish all hatred and love of power in the world and in the hearts of all men.' And Mother Teresa did just this by often being the first to reach areas devastated by natural causes or human conflict.

In August 1982, she set out for Beirut. She had heard that several crippled children were trapped in a hospital which had been damaged in the crossfire. Despite repeated reminders from well-wishers that she might be in the line of fire, Mother made up her mind to fetch the children the next day.

'Tomorrow there will be a truce—fighting will stop,' she said.

The Sisters prayed all night that there might be a truce the next day.

And so there was.

'We took charge of the orphaned and crippled children and brought them safely home,' Mother told her story to a wide-eyed tremulous gathering. 'We were lacking in almost everything. Some young people, among them Muslims, Christians and Druses, came to help us, and the smallest went home to bring their clothes to give to these children. One of them was chewing gum and in a burst of love, he took the gum out of his mouth and gave it to a little one.'

On a more serious note she concluded, 'God has His own ways and means to work in the hearts of men and we do not know how close they are to Him.'

'We Stay'

On her travels to the Middle East and the Holy Land,
Mother passed through Gaza. The area was a hotbed
of discontent and rivalries causing frequent bloodshed.
There was no peace. Thus it was a chosen area for the
Sisters to exercise their ministry of love and charity. They
were to be instruments of God's peace in the world, for,
as Mother said, 'works of love are works of peace.'

When she received an invitation to open a house in
Gaza, Mother immediately accepted. She needed a Superior
with a strong faith and an adventurous spirit,
afraid of no one, conversant with Arabic or able to learn
it quickly.

Mother chose a Sister who had joined her at the
very beginning, who had known the heroic years. The
Sisters chosen to go to Gaza would be helped by the
prayers of all at Mother House. As they were leaving,
they prayed together, and Mother blessed them. The
whole community sang a hymn entrusting them to
God.

When the Sisters arrived in Gaza they were taken
to the parish house where they were supposed to live.
As they entered the main room they were met by a
caretaker who merely said, 'The parish priest who was
living here was killed yesterday in this room. You can

see the bloodstains on the wall. Are you going to stay here?'

The Sisters held their breath as the Superior in an act of faith answered: 'We stay.'

A Contract with Jesus

Mother Teresa never lost her sense of humour and she did not usually complain but one day she told her Sisters: 'Everyday I have to sign so many letters, sometimes I feel tired. So I have made a contract with Jesus.'

Mother always prefixed her signature with 'God bless you' and then signed 'M Teresa MC'. M stands for Mary. All the Sisters are first Mary and then the name that they are called. MC is the abbreviation for Missionaries of Charity. The letters add up to twenty and Mother said she offered up as many acts of love for that person to whom the letter was addressed.

It was the same story when the cameras clicked. Mother said that one of the few things that she hated was having her photograph taken. But she made use of everything 'for the glory of God.' She told Jesus that whenever she allowed herself to be photographed, he must take one soul out of purgatory to heaven.

The Joy of Sharing

A lady wearing a very expensive sari and accessories entered Mother House looking a little uncomfortable and feeling out of place. She waited in the parlour and as soon as Mother entered, she rushed towards her saying, 'Mother, I want to share your work.'

Mother prayed for a moment for inspiration to be able to convey to the lady, without appearing critical of her lifestyle, the true spirit of sharing in her work. She said to her, 'I would begin with your sari. You start by buying a cheaper sari the next time, and the money you save, you bring to me for the poor.'

So the woman started to buy cheaper saris and each time she bought one, she would bring the money that she had saved to Mother Teresa. The lady said, 'It has changed my life. I have really understood what it is to share. I have received much more than I have given.'

There came a time when that same lady came dressed in such cheap saris that one day Mother Teresa called her aside and gently admonished her saying that she should not overdo this sharing.

Always for Others

The whole of her life Mother Teresa asked for things material, and services, but never for herself. She always wanted them for others. This act of faith was noticed and it made many people help her willingly.

She once related how at the beginning of her career she went to a wholesale chemist shop, and gave the owner a piece of paper with a long list of medicines, saying, 'I need these medicines for the poor.' He answered, 'Lady, you have come to the wrong house; but let me finish my work.'

Mother sat down and prayed her rosary whilst the owner did his book work. After a long time he looked up and saw Mother praying with her head down and asked, 'Lady, what are you doing?'

'I am praying for you,' she answered, 'that you may give the medicines for the poor.'

'Alright, come here,' he said, and gave her all the medicines she needed.

Dr B.C. Roy, the chief minister of West Bengal, used to give free medical advice early in the morning. Several times, Mother went to sit with the crowd of patients. When her turn came, she asked the chief minister for water or electricity for one slum or another. He told his secretary to take note and see to it. Of course it was done.

One day Dr Roy remarked, 'Mother, you always ask me for other people, never for yourself. You may come to my office at any time, I will always receive you.'

In those heroic days of the first years of the Missionaries of Charity, Mother went to restaurants and shops asking, 'Have you any broken biscuits for the children?' and she collected the bits of biscuits they kept for her.

Many years later, when she had become famous, she received cases of biscuits from manufacturers in India, Holland and Germany. They were still for the children, the sick and the old persons.

To Cure an Ulcer

A priest met Mother in the small parlour at Mother House. 'I have an ulcer,' he said, 'a duodenal ulcer, and the surgeon says I should be operated upon.' Mother reacted quickly and strongly, 'No operation!' She spoke like a person accustomed to command. 'No operation! Milk and biscuits. Drink plenty of milk, it is an antacid, and eat biscuits whenever your stomach is empty. No sugar, no fat, no fruits, eat only boiled food. And carry biscuits in your pocket to eat between meals, because the empty stomach makes acid. Also, keep some biscuits close to your bed and eat one when you wake up at night. Like that you will get rid of your ulcer. We have some very good biscuits from Holland sent by our friends.

'Sister Agnes,' Mother called, 'Give Father some Dutch biscuits for his ulcer.' Sister Agnes soon came back with a large bag filled with good strong biscuits. Mother added, 'You have milk powder, that will do. Take these biscuits and get cured.'

This was practical wisdom. Mother Teresa was remembering the teaching received many years earlier, during her stay with the American Medical Missionary Sisters at the Patna hospital. Three months later, the priest told Mother: 'Thank you, Mother, the ulcer has gone.'

Prayer and a Passport

Mother found a young man resting his tired body against the outer boundary wall of a house in Calcutta. He looked totally lost. Mother took him to one of her homes. A few hours later, she returned to talk to him and came to know that he was a foreigner; he was very highly educated but had fallen into bad company and his passport had been stolen. Mother asked him what had made him leave his family and his home and come to India. He said that from childhood his father had never looked him in the eye and had not wanted him. When he grew up, he felt that his father was jealous of him.

Mother was a very pragmatic person and she realized the seriousness of his situation. She left no stone unturned to ensure that all the formalities were completed so that the man could get a passport and return home to make his reconciliation. But whenever she narrated this incident, she made no mention of her role in this part of the story.

'After much praying,' Mother said, 'the Sisters helped him to return home and to forgive his father. This was helpful to both of them.'

The Missing Drop in the Ocean

A friend of Mother Teresa from her early days came by hoping to have a quiet word with her and found, to her pleasant surprise, that there were few visitors that afternoon. She sat down on the old wooden bench in the covered passageway between the nuns' quarters and the chapel.

It had been a long time since they met and there was much to talk about. The friend poured out her frustration that her efforts to help seemed to make no difference at all to the quality of lives of thousands of poor people. Mother placed her strong work-worn hand on hers and said, 'We ourselves feel that what we are doing is just a drop in the ocean. But if that drop was not in the ocean, I think the ocean would be less because of the missing drop.'

Challenged by her friend that there must be bigger and better ways of helping the poor, Mother Teresa answered, 'I do not agree with the big way of doing things. What matters is the individual. If we wait till we get the numbers, then we will be lost in the numbers and we will never be able to show that love and respect for the person.'

Christmas and the Family

$\mathcal{M}$other Teresa wrote to her co-workers at Christmas in 1995:

'Some of the children in our homes in Calcutta were given an early Christmas treat one year by an international airline which gave them a free one-hour ride. I wish you could have seen the excitement of these hundred and fifty children, looking so neat in matching shirts and caps that had been donated for the occasion. How wonderful that our handicapped and malnourished and abandoned children, who would otherwise never have experienced the joy of flying, were given the chance.'

Mother concluded the newsletter with a part of the message she had sent to the World Conference on Women in Beijing:

'Instead of death and sorrow, let us bring peace and joy to the world. To do this we must beg God for His gift of peace and learn to love and accept each other as brothers and sisters, children of God. We know that the best place for children to learn how to love and to pray is in the family, by seeing the love and prayer of their mother and father. . . . When families are strong and united, children can see God's special love in the love of their father and mother and can grow to make their country a loving, prayerful place.'

Be Somebody to Somebody

The large well-appointed sitting room in a well-to-do lady's apartment was already crowded. It was 9.30 a. m., early for society ladies, but this was a very special occasion. Mother Teresa was coming to talk to them. Mother sometimes met groups in one of their homes and the only refreshment offered by the hostess on such occasions was a glass of water. This was Mother's wish.

Mother arrived accompanied by a Sister and greeted the ladies with folded hands. Everyone was eager to hear Mother speak. She wasted no time and began:

'We all want to love God. But how? Where? Jesus taught us and he said, "Whatever you do to the least of my brethren you do to me."

'At the end of life we are going to be judged on the basis of our love for one another, on what we have been to the hungry, to the naked, to the homeless.

'What is this hunger? Is it the hunger of Africa and India, of all the people hungry for a piece of bread, for a plate of rice? It's also the hunger for love. Hunger to be loved by somebody. To be somebody to somebody. The terrible thing is to be unwanted.

'One day I was walking down the streets of London and saw a man sitting all alone, looking so terribly lonely. I walked up to him and took his hand and shook it. As my hand is very warm, he exclaimed, "Oh! After so long, this is the first time I've felt the warmth of a human hand." And then his face brightened up. He was a different being. The warmth of a human hand was a small thing, but through it he felt that there was somebody who really wanted him, somebody who really cared. I never realized before that such a small action could bring so much joy.'

Prince Charles

Kings, presidents, heads of state, and many eminent persons have talked to, and played with the children at Shishu Bhavans in many countries. Some have cradled and cuddled the little ones in their arms.

Just after Christmas in 1980, Prince Charles made a twenty-four-hour halt in Calcutta. He met Mother Teresa at Shishu Bhavan. She introduced him to the newest member of her family, a baby who had been abandoned somewhere in the city. Mother took him to the chapel and they prayed together for ten minutes.

Mother said, 'He was impressed. I gave him a card with the prayer of Saint Francis of Assisi and asked him to say it everyday. As he was about to leave, I turned to the Prince and said, "I cannot do what you can do and you cannot do what I can do, but the two of us together can do something beautiful for God." '

The Joy of Insecurity

On her way home to India after her first visit to Canada, Mother Teresa was sitting in the transit lounge at Heathrow airport telling her rosary. A journalist spotted her and managed to get to her and the volley of questions began.

How was she received in Canada?

Mother looked up and there was no trace of annoyance at being rudely interrupted in her prayers. She answered as though she had been waiting to be asked, 'There were twenty-five thousand people at the rally. In Montreal, three or four people came forward to give me a house. It was so beautiful! One man took me around to see the houses and he said, "Even if you don't take one of them, I can sell one and buy you the one you want." Now we have five houses. People are very happy to have the Sisters there.

'They asked if they could give $10,000 a month, but I said that we would lose the joy of insecurity and dependence on Divine Providence.'

The Dignity of the Poor

The greatest injustice we have done to our poor people is that we think they are good for nothing; we have forgotten to treat them with respect, with dignity as a child of God.'

This story narrated by Mother Teresa was proof of what she had just said.

'One day, a young boy, fifteen or sixteen years old, came crying and begged me to give him some soap. I knew that the family of the boy had been rich and had become poor. He said to me, "My sister goes to high school and every day she is sent back because her sari is not washed and we do not have any soap to wash it. Please give me some soap so that she can wash her sari and she can go to school and finish her education." Now see the humiliation the family had to suffer because they were poor. We should treat them not with pity, but compassion.'

Helping Mother Teresa's Way

A woman was so overwhelmed by Mother's words that she slipped off her gold bangles from her wrists and offered them to Mother. Restraining her, Mother told her this story.

'A rich man came to me and said, "I have a big house in Holland. Do you want me to give it up?"

'I said, "No."

' "Do you want me to live in that house?"

'I said, "Yes."

' "I have a big car; do you want me to give that up instead?"

'I said, "No. But what I want you to do is to go back and see more of the lonely people who live in Holland. Then, every now and then I want you to bring a few of them at a time and entertain them. Bring them in that car of yours and let them enjoy a few hours in your beautiful house. Then your big house will become a centre of love—full of light, full of joy, full of life."

'He smiled and said he would be so happy to bring the people to his home but that he wanted to give up something in his life. So, I suggested: "When you go to the store to buy a new suit or some clothes, instead of buying the best, buy something a little cheaper and use that extra money to buy something for somebody else, or better still for the poor." When I finished, he looked amazed and exclaimed, "Oh! Is that the way Mother? I never thought of it." '

'The Poor Are Always with Us'

*H*elpers and volunteers used to gather around Mother Teresa before they went out to work in her homes, and sometimes on their return. Some were searching for a direction and to them she would say: 'Discover through direct contact. Go to the Home for the Dying, and learn your lessons not out of a book, but in the rough-and-tumble of life, among real people, in a setting you will never forget.' She remembered a young man who had spent a day at Nirmal Hriday and returned to ask for his next assignment. She said:

'One morning, I was working when a Sister came in and said, "A tourist wants to see you; he is the same person who came the other day."

'I said: "Tell him to go and work in Kalighat." The Sister replied that he said he had gone there the previous day. "Yes," I said, "he can go again today; the poor are still there."'

Openness to All Faiths

A Korean girl, a Buddhist, came to work as a volunteer with the Missionaries of Charity in 1989. Her dream was to qualify as a doctor and return to work with Mother Teresa. The time had come for her to proceed to the United States for medical studies. All the arrangements for her visa were completed but she was in trouble. An official of the US Consulate suddenly declared that he would not issue the visa unless she brought a Sister with her. He would not accept a written certificate. Desperate, she went to Mother House and was told that the Sisters were too busy with their work to accompany her. Mother was then out of Calcutta.

The girl came to Saint Xavier's College to seek advice from a frequent visitor to Mother House. When Mother returned after a few days he spoke to her. She most readily agreed to help, and sent a Sister along with the girl.

Impressed by the girl's vibrant sincerity, he suggested to Mother, 'Why don't you open a branch of your Sisters' Congregation for such sincere persons of other faiths? They would work along with your Sisters and have the same lifestyle. They would be fully open to the spirit of the Gospel and to Christ, but many do not want to change their own religion. They could also bring the best of their own spiritual tradition.'

He expected Mother to smile and ignore his hare-brained scheme. But without batting an eyelid, she answered, 'I have already thought of it and have spoken to the Holy Father about it. He told me to go ahead.'

Doesn't God Spoil Us?

Someone wanted to give some money to Mother Teresa but was told, 'Why give it to Mother Teresa who will use it for people who are dying, or for lepers who are useless to society? Instead, invest it in a course or seminar where it can be used for youth education or to support families.'

Mother Teresa's reply to this was: 'Yes, we work for the hopeless and the helpless of society, for those who are good for nothing, for we see in them the image of God.' She was aware that 'India needs plans and coordinated action; that India needs technicians, skilled men, economists, doctors, nurses for her development.' But, she asked, 'How long would we have to wait for those plans to produce results? We do not know. Meanwhile people have to live, they have to be given food to eat, be taken care of and dressed. Our field of work is India today.'

Mother said, 'While these needs continue, our work will continue.'

On another occasion, Mother told her Sisters how she dealt with similar remarks at a seminar in Bangalore where a delegate stood up and said to her, 'Mother Teresa, you are spoiling the poor people by giving them things free. They are losing their human dignity. You should take at least ten paise for what you give them; then they will feel their human dignity more.'

A murmur rose in the hall. When everyone was quiet, Mother Teresa said calmly, 'No one is spoiling us as much as God Himself. See the wonderful gifts He has given us freely. None of you here has no glasses on, yet you can all see. Say, if God were to take money for your sight, what would happen? We are spending so much money in Shishu Bhavan to buy oxygen for saving life, yet continually we are breathing and living on oxygen and we do not pay anything for it.'

There was a profound silence. Nobody spoke a word after that.

A Piece of Chocolate

Mother Teresa had plenty of experience in coping with disasters and her reactions were always prompt. 'We know what people need and many organizations and people come forward to give and to help and the work goes on.' When people heard of the terrible famine in Ethiopia and that Mother Teresa was off to Addis Ababa, foodstuff began to pour into Mother House. The Sisters and volunteers were busy sorting and packing tins of milk, packets of sugar, rice and flour into old cardboard cartons.

Mother Teresa often talked about the sacrifice children make for children—the children in England sacrificed a slice of bread and jam each; the children in Denmark, a glass of milk and the children in India a rasgulla for their less fortunate brothers and sisters.

She said, 'The children of Calcutta had come to know from the Sisters how much the children are suffering in Ethiopia. And they came and each one gave something very, very small—money or something. Whatever they had, they gave. A little boy came to me and said: "I have no money, I have nothing but I have this piece of chocolate. Take this with you and give it to the children of Ethiopia."

'That little child loved with a great love because I think it was the first time that he had been given a piece of chocolate in his hand and he gave it with joy to be able to share. He gave it to remove a little suffering of someone in faraway Ethiopia.

'This is the joy of loving. To give until it hurts.'

'You Are My Budget'

*M*oney?' says Mother, 'I never think of it. It always comes. If God wants a work to be done, He sends the means. If He does not give the means, He does not want that work. So, why worry?'

In her lifetime money came abundantly and often unexpectedly.

One day, the director of a large multinational company from Mumbai came to Calcutta and called on Mother. After introducing himself as Mr Thomas, he said:

'Mother, may I ask you what your budget is for the next year?'

Mother answered, 'I have no budget. How can I know at the beginning of the year how many Mr Thomases, how many Mrs Thomases, how many Miss Thomases will come and tell me, "We have a property we wish to hand over to the Missionaries of Charity"? So I make no budget. You are my budget.'

Mr Thomas then explained that his multinational company had a large warehouse in the centre of Mumbai. They wished to shift to another area and they were considering donating the property to the Missionaries of Charity.

Some time later the donation was effected. Mother had previously received a similar gift in the east of Calcutta from another multinational and had called it Prem Daan, or Gift of Love. The Mumbai property was called Asha Daan, or Gift of Hope.

The Extended Family

Mother Teresa's work among the poorest of the poor is associated in many people's minds with washing the wounds of leprosy patients, feeding the hungry, rescuing unwanted babies and collecting the dying off the streets. Many ask how they can help.

Here is the story of a 'big company' whose employees were motivated to become involved in Mother's work in Mumbai by their boss.

'I went with the head of a big company to his factory in Mumbai where over three thousand people were working. He had started a scheme among them where they all gave something to feed the people in Asha Daan, our home. I had gone there to thank them and to my surprise I found that many were disabled.

'I was really struck by the thoughtfulness of this very busy man. He knew nearly all the workers by name and while he showed me around, I noticed that he greeted each one and asked them about their families on a personal note.

'Thoughtfulness comes when there is true love. Never be so busy as not to think of others.'

'Pray For Me'

In 1985, Mother Teresa visited China and for many days after she returned she spoke about her meeting with the senior Chinese leader Deng Xiaoping and his son. They showed her a home for the handicapped that Deng Xiaoping was supervising. Mother praised his work as 'truly God's work' to which he said that since he did not believe in God, how could he do God's work? She answered, 'You are doing the work of charity and that is for God. Pray for me and I will pray for you.'

A Last Wish

In 1994, Mother Teresa visited Shanghai. The eighty-three-year-old Nobel Laureate emerged from the airport helping to push her own baggage cart piled high with brown cardboard cartons tied with rope. By now, airlines throughout the world had learnt to recognize Mother Teresa's luggage and treated it as VIP cargo!

The main purpose of her visit was to meet Deng Pufang, head of the Chinese Federation for the Disabled. Deng himself had been severely injured during the Cultural Revolution and was confined to a wheelchair. Asked what she intended to do during her stay, Mother said, 'Help the poor.'

Mother Teresa's great desire was to open a home for the poor in China and in 1997, a few months before she died, she said, 'We shall go to China.' That she was not able to fulfill this wish was her last regret.

'God Still Loves Us'

Mother had come to the Home for the Dying in Kalighat, Calcutta. She noticed that a tourist was standing and watching her. When she finished her work, she went up and greeted him. He told her, 'I came here with so much hate in my heart, hate for God, hate for man. I came here empty, faithless, embittered and I saw a Sister giving her wholehearted attention to that patient there and I realized that God still lives. Now I go out a different man. I believe there is a God and He loves us still.'

Mother repeated this incident at one of her talks. She said, 'I want this to be imprinted on your minds that God loves the world through you and through me.'

The Breakfast TV Show

Once Mother Teresa made an appearance on a morning television show in America.

This was the first time Mother had been in a television studio and she was unprepared for the many interruptions for commercials. The colours on the monitor screen were also disturbing and the interviewer's green hair, mauve nose and pink moustache took her by surprise.

As it happened, that particular morning the commercials were all about different varieties of packaged bread and other foods commended to viewers as being non-fattening and with plenty of roughage which has no nutritive value. It took a little time for the irony to strike home, for Mother's constant preoccupation was to find the wherewithal to nourish the starving and put a little flesh on their skeletal frames. When it did, Mother was heard to remark in a quiet but perfectly audible voice: 'I see that Christ is needed in television studios.'

It was an unprecedented occurrence. A sudden silence descended on the studio and the floor manager was struck dumb. Actually, as the commercials were still running, Mother Teresa was not on the air but her remark rated a mention in the *New York Times*.

'Thank You'

*M*other Teresa would sometimes reminisce about her experiences in the streets and slums of the cities where she began her work. On one occasion, she told a story illustrating a lesson she had been taught by a woman who was materially poor but spiritually rich.

'One evening, we went out and picked up four people from the street and one of them was in a most terrible condition. I told the Sisters: "You take care of the other three; I will take care of the one who looks the worst." So I did for her all that my love can do. I put her in bed and there was such a beautiful smile on her face. She took hold of my hand as she said one word only: "thank you," and she died.

'I could not but examine my conscience before her. And I asked: what would I say if I were in her place? And my answer was very simple. I would have tried to draw a little attention to myself. I would have said: "I am hungry, I am dying, I am cold, I am in pain." But she gave me much more. She gave me her grateful love. And she died with a smile on her face.'

God's Bank Gone Bust

*M*other had a long list of invitations sent by cardinals, archbishops and bishops from all over the world, begging her to come and bring her Sisters to work in their dioceses. It was New York's turn and Mother arrived with two Sisters. She began exploring the most depressed areas to discover the nature of help that was needed and whether she could fulfil that need. She said, 'In one of the houses, a woman living alone was dead many days before she was found, and she was only found because her body had begun to decompose. The people around did not even know her name. It is being unwanted that is the worst disease that any human being can ever experience.'

Cardinal Cooke, who had invited Mother to New York, thought that perhaps it was money that was the crux of Mother's problem in making a start. So he offered to pay, it is reported, $500 a month for each Sister working in Harlem. One can only imagine the look on Mother's face when the offer was conveyed to her. She replied, 'Do you think that God is bankrupt in New York? He provides the means. So why do we worry?'

A Ticket to Heaven

$\mathcal{A}$ group of teachers from the United States was touring India. In Calcutta, a visit to Mother Teresa was first on their itinerary.

They stood before the small door, the entrance to Mother House. A chain hangs down through a hole and a tug on it serves the purpose of a calling bell. Beside the door, there is a wooden board on which the words 'MOTHER TERESA' are painted with an indicator to show whether she is in or out. That morning she was in.

At the end of a lively conversation with Mother, they asked, 'Tell us something that will help us to live our lives better. What do you think we could do to bring peace and joy into the world?'

With a big smile Mother said: 'Smile at each other. Smile at your husband, smile at your wife, smile at your children, be happy with your children. It doesn't matter who it is, smile at them.'

Mother Teresa could be the butt of her own jokes and laugh at herself. At dinner, that night, she told the Sisters about her American visitors. She said, 'Because I talk so much about giving with a smile, and sometimes I look serious, one of them asked me, "Are you married?" And I said: "Yes, and sometimes I find it very difficult to smile at my spouse, Jesus, because he can be very demanding. This is really true and here is where love comes in. Even when it is demanding we give it with joy." '

Mother said that being constantly in the limelight was 'one of the most demanding things.' So she had made a pact with her God. She said to Jesus, 'If I don't go to heaven for anything else, I will be going to heaven for all the travelling and all the publicity, because it has purified me and made me really ready to go to heaven.'

'Now I Believe'

Many young foreigners come to work as volunteers with the Missionaries of Charity in their homes for the poor during a few weeks or months or even a year or two.

'A young Frenchman came to me,' said Mother. 'He was working with the Sisters. He told me, "I have lost my Catholic faith. I have no belief in God any more." I told him, "Read this book" and gave him *Remain in My Love—the Meditations on the Gospel of St. John.* He took it and went away.

'Three weeks later the young Frenchman came back and returned the book. "Now I believe," he said.

'Isn't that beautiful?' said Mother to an old-timer to whom she was narrating the story.

'Yes, Mother, and of course you had prayed for the young man?' he asked.

Love For God in Action

$\mathcal{D}$uring an interview with Mother Teresa, two Japanese gentlemen expressed their feeling that many of the Japanese people might hesitate to seek help at her home because it was a Christian institution. 'It has a cross,' one of them said, 'and the cross is an obstacle to many in Japan. People might look at the cross and they might hesitate to come because they are not Christians.'

Mother told them about the most joyful place she had ever visited and dispelled their fears.

'In Calcutta, we have a Home for the Dying near the great temple of the Hindu goddess Kali. It is one of the most famous temples in India and we have the home for the sick and the dying next door. They know we are Christians and we help them die in peace with their God. When the Hindus die, we call the Hindus and they take the bodies; when the Muslims die, the Muslims take the bodies; when the Buddhists die, the Buddhists take the bodies; when the Christians die, the Christians come and take the bodies. But there is no fear. By being in the institution there, what we have to prove to our suffering people through our actions is that God loves them.

'Our love for God in action is our service to the poor. Your love for God in action is to write properly. Your love for God is to write the truth, to spread goodness, to spread beautiful things. This is the way you put your love for God in action.'

Shut-in and Forgotten

*M*other Teresa coined her own word for unwanted people. She called them 'shut-ins'.

She often repeated one of her traumatic experiences.

'I visited a home where they kept the old parents of sons and daughters who had put them into this institution and perhaps forgotten about them. These old people had everything—good food, a comfortable place, television—but every one was looking towards the door. And I did not see a single smile on their faces. I turned to Sister and asked, "Why are they not smiling?" I am used to seeing a smile on the faces of our people; even the dying ones smile. Sister said, "It is like this nearly every day. They are hoping and expecting that a son or daughter will come and visit them."

'It is this neglect to love that brings spiritual poverty.'

Mother Meets the Pope

*I*n 1992 all the Belgian bishops signed a petition to the Vatican asking that Father Damian De Veuster, known as the Apostle of the Lepers, be beatified.

Father Damian, a Belgian priest, had volunteered to go to Hawaii and work on the island of Molokai among the leprosy patients. He stayed there till he died, doing spiritual work for the leprosy patients. When he contracted the disease he said happily, 'Now I can pray to God saying, "We lepers." '

The Belgian bishops' petition went to Rome. The answer arrived in two Latin words—*non constant:* the holiness of Father Damian is not proved, so there can be no beatification.

Some time later, Mother asked Pope John Paul II, 'Are you not going to beatify Father Damian? It would encourage all those who work among the leprosy patients, as many in the Missionaries of Charity do.' The Pope answered, 'He worked no miracles.'

'Do you require miracles to beatify a priest who gave his life to serve the lepers? And he did work miracles; now no one is afraid to touch a leper for they know the disease is not contagious.' Mother said.

The Pope said nothing.

A few months later the Belgian bishops received a letter from the Vatican ordering them to 'prepare everything for the beatification of Father Damian De Veuster next year.' Mother had done it.

Pope John Paul had intimated that he would proceed to the beatification only if Mother Teresa was present, 'because the people will not come for Father Damian but they will come to see Mother.'

And so it happened that the Holy Father gave to the leprosy patients and those who tend them, a patron in heaven they may pray to.

Mother's Suku Remembers: 1

Suku was an abandoned child on the streets of Calcutta. Forty-three years ago, Mother Teresa carried him in her arms to her newly-founded home for children. He was identified as 'Mother's Suku', especially when he was in trouble. He was older than he looked and was unable to walk, but his handicap did not come in the way of his being the naughtiest child in Mother's first batch of seven boys at the home.

'Mother was our mother, collectively and individually. I was very naughty. I'd pull her sari and run into her room whenever we were taken to Mother House,' Suku remembers.

'When I was sixteen, Mother said to me, "Come and serve the people" and took me with her to the Home for the Dying. That particular morning, I found everyone in the home holding their noses and I soon realized why. A putrid smell was coming from a man who had just been admitted. One of his lower limbs was wrapped in a dirty bloodstained cloth. Mother immediately sized up the situation and asked me to open the bandage. I approached the man but before I could touch him I felt so sick, I went to Mother. She opened the bandage, cleaned the wound and put a clean dressing on his leg. I was watching her from a distance and after a while, it was not Mother I saw; it was an angel. My vision was broken by

Mother's voice calling me. "Now you can come, Suku, and sit beside him." She picked up the soiled and stinking bandages and disposed of them herself.

'I tell my children often about this wonderful experience of my life.'

Suku is now forty-five years old and has his own family and a small house which he has named Nirmala Bhavan.

Mother's Suku Remembers: 2

Suku was ready to do anything that Mother Teresa asked him to do except go to school. He knew that what she wanted most of all was for him to study and make something of his life. But Suku was a school drop-out. To please Mother, he agreed to take vocational training and was admitted to one of the best technical schools in West Bengal.

One morning, he ran away and came to Mother House. Suku was to forget all his own problems by what he saw that morning while waiting for an opportunity to grab hold of Mother and cry on her shoulder. He saw that Mother was surrounded by many 'big' people and settled down in a corner to wait until they had gone.

Out of the corner of her eye, Mother must have seen a poor old man sitting on the cement bench outside the parlour. She excused herself and went out to meet him. When Mother spoke in Bengali she used to address old people as Ma or Baba—mother or father—and young people as *cheley* or *meyey*—son or daughter.

She addressed the old man in Bengali: 'Baba, what do you want?'

'Is it possible to meet Ma Teresa;'

'I am that *meyey*,' Mother said.

Untying a small knotted bundle which was slung over his shoulder, he offered her some *moori* or puffed rice—

the poor man's snack. Suku was watching Mother intently as she cupped both her hands and received the puffed rice as if it were the most precious gift on earth.

Suku felt a change come over him. He returned and finished his course at the technical school and now works as a Grade I technician in the State Government Electricity Board.

After Retirement—What?

At Washington D.C., after the president of the United States had honoured her with a Medal of Freedom, Mother Teresa was interviewed. One of the questions she was asked was, 'Mother, when you are no longer Superior General, what will you do?'

Mother answered, 'I can do many things. For instance, I am quite good at cleaning toilets and I am good at cleaning drains . . . For me to speak to the president of the United States or to clean toilets and drains, it is all my service to Jesus. I do whatever he wants me to do.'

Now I Am Nothing

The General Chapter held in 1997 elected Sister Nirmala as the successor to Mother Teresa as Superior General of the Missionaries of Charity. Later, Mother took her to Rome and in a private audience at the Vatican, she introduced the new Superior General to Pope John Paul.

The Holy Father blessed Sister Nirmala and gave her some good advice. When he had finished, Mother Teresa exclaimed: 'Now I am nothing.'

Pope John Paul replied: 'You are the foundress.'

He had the last word, for that glorious title no one could ever take away from her.

That cry 'I am nothing' proved to be an outburst of wit or humour rather short-lived, for soon Mother was off flying to the United States to visit every one of the houses she had opened there.

She was back to inspecting, questioning, advising and directing the Sisters with all her practical wisdom. After more than a month she returned to Rome to tell Pope John Paul what she had seen and done.

The Pope's words certainly remained on her mind. A Sister recalls that two days before her death, Mother was laughing and joking at dinner with some Sisters and said, 'I am an ordinary Sister.' Then she put her index finger before her lips, closed her eyes and said quietly, 'The Holy Father said, "You are the foundress.' "

The Mango Tree

The family next door to Shishu Bhavan in Calcutta looked with apprehension at their new neighbours in white saris with blue borders. The original colonial style bungalow next door was soon hidden by ugly concrete additions, no doubt functional.

Rumours emanated that a hospital, or a destitute home or frighteningly, a leprosy centre, was in the making. The family was happy to see a home for orphaned children grow instead. Then in the early seventies, a member of the family noticed a temporary structure was being constructed using their common boundary wall without their permission. The head of the family did not waste any time in reporting the matter to the civic authorities.

Late one evening, when the young residents of Shishu Bhavan had gone to bed, Mother sat talking to some friends. She said that a few days earlier she had felt that something was amiss and had set about rectifying the lapse. She paid a visit to her angry neighbour. 'It's strange that we haven't met before,' she said and he began to soften. She spoke of her work with the poor and her dependence on the contractors who were doing the building work. She personally took him on a conducted tour of the home and before he left, offered to dismantle the offending structure. He could only mumble something to the effect that the same mistake should not be repeated.

Good relations were restored until a ball thrown by one of the children in the home broke his window-panes. The incident brought him into another confrontation which left him feeling a little mean as the children were forbidden to play ball games after that.

A decade later, an adjoining plot owned by his cousin was sold to the Missionaries of Charity and was converted into a playground and, thankfully, not another building. In order to accommodate a slide for the children, a hundred-and-twenty-year-old mango tree had to be cut down. The woodcutters arrived and the old man decided to go the next day to ask Mother Teresa to intervene. But she died that night, and the tree was felled.

Courtesy: The Statesman Ltd.

'I Will Not'

Mother Teresa narrated to a friend this story which has not been previously made known to the public.

Mother and another Sister were travelling to the Holy Land and on reaching the Control Point, they were stopped by a woman police officer. Previously, a woman dressed as a Christian nun had been found with a small gun under her clothes so the security officers on duty had become extremely strict. Every woman was required to strip so as to show she carried no arms.

The officer told Mother, 'Go into that small room and strip.'

Mother answered, 'No, I will not.' The officer repeated her order. Mother again forcibly said, '*I will not.*'

And it remained at that. Finally, she was allowed to enter the Holy Land through that checkpoint.

Mother ended the story saying, 'Thanks be to God.'

God Never Makes a Mistake

A Sister who was one of the first to join Mother Teresa, was asked what struck her most in Mother's character. She answered, 'Her faith.'

'I take the Lord at His word,' Mother used to say.

In August 1996, Mother was seriously ill in a nursing home in Calcutta, just a few days before her birthday. She had lived through a critical night and when a Sister came to see her in the morning, Mother looked at her and said, 'I don't know what God is doing. He knows. We cannot understand, but one thing I'm sure of: God never makes a mistake.'

Mother returned to Mother House. A short while later, she was admitted to a well-known heart centre in the city. At about the same time, Sister Agnes, her student and the first aspirant to the Missionaries of Charity, had a setback after remission from cancer. She prayed that her own life may be taken and Mother's spared so that she could complete her work. Sister Agnes died and Mother regained her strength, and was able to visit her homes in the United States of America.

Her successor as Superior General was elected in early 1997 and received her blessing. Mother Teresa passed away on 5 September 1997 and was laid to rest in Mother House, Calcutta.